'2/00

32.00

Kansas

AMERICA THE BEAUTIFUL
second series

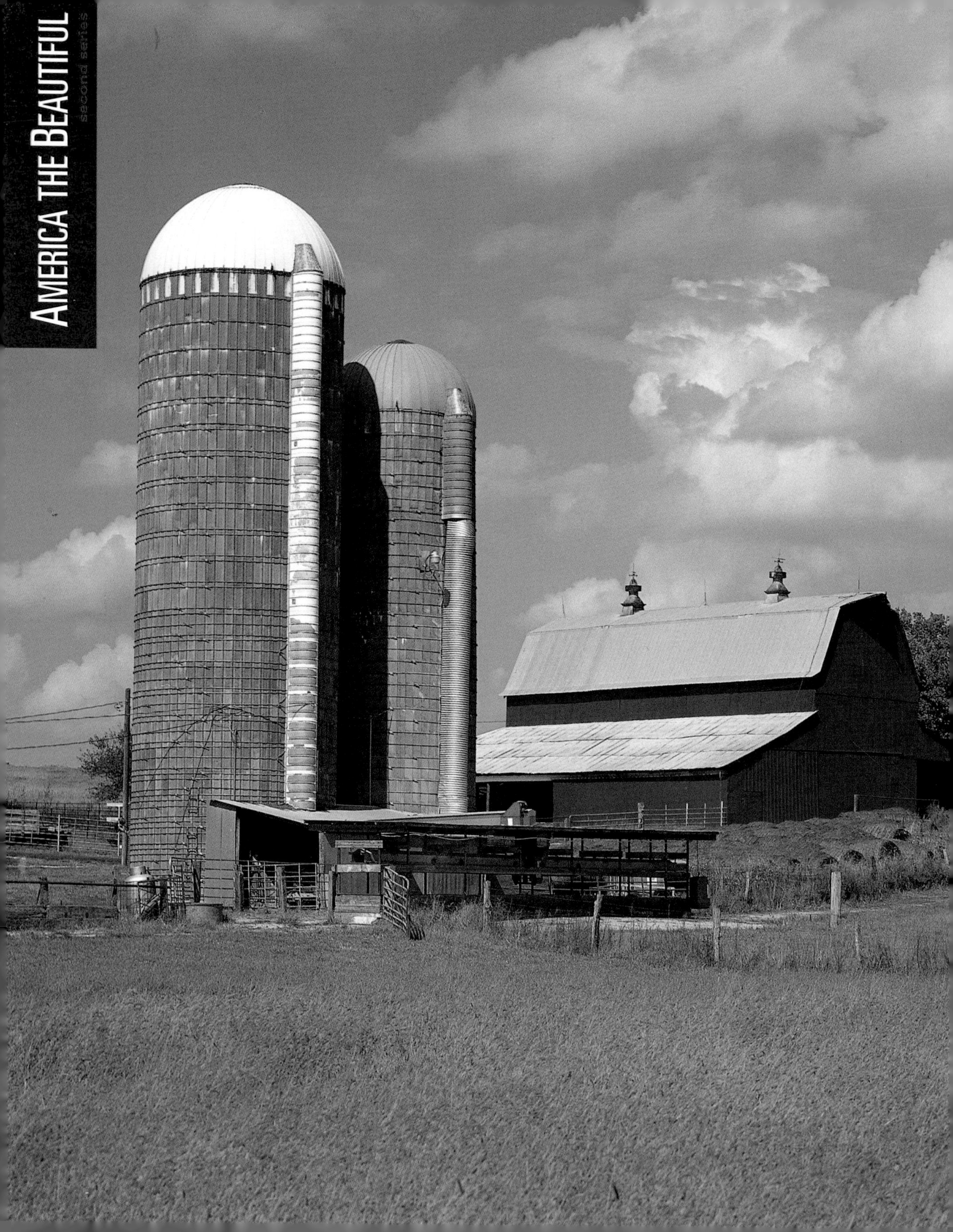

Kansas

Nancy Robinson Masters

Children's Press®
A Division of Grolier Publishing
New York   London   Hong Kong   Sydney
Danbury, Connecticut

Frontispiece: A farm near Holton

Front cover: A Kansas sorghum farm

Back cover: Downtown Wichita

Consultant: Roy Bird, Kansas State Library

Please note: All statistics are as up-to-date as possible at the time of publication.

Visit Children's Press on the Internet at http://publishing.grolier.com

Book production by Editorial Directions, Inc.

Library of Congress Cataloging-in-Publication Data

Robinson Masters, Nancy.
    Kansas / Nancy Robinson Masters.
      144 p. 24 cm. — (America the beautiful. Second series)
    Includes bibliographical references and indexes.
    Summary : Describes the geography, plants, animals, history, economy, religions,
culture, sports, arts, and people of Kansas.
    ISBN 0-516-20993-0
    1. Kansas—Juvenile literature. [1. Kansas.] I. Title. II. Series.
F226.3.B57 1998
978.1—dc21
                                        99-12210
                                          CIP
                                          AC

Acknowledgments

The author sincerely appreciates the assistance provided by the Office of the Governor of the State of Kansas, the University of Kansas, and researcher Ruth Sellers.

Cheyenne Bottoms
Wildlife Area

The Konza Prairie

Monument Rocks

Contents

Sunflower

Bison

A Kansas tornado

Geographic center

Ornate box turtle

CHAPTER ONE

Kansas Sunshine

essie Spencer was homesick. She handed a cup of coffee and a doughnut to the soldier standing in line at the American Red Cross canteen in Brest, France. It was 1918, and her thoughts were thousands of miles away from the battlefields of Europe. Jessie's hometown of Fredonia, Kansas, was preparing to celebrate Kansas Day.

Native Americans hunted buffalo and made their homes in what is now Kansas.

Each year, Kansas Day honors the anniversary of the day the state of Kansas was admitted to the Union. On January 29, 1918, as World War I dragged on in Europe, Kansans celebrated fifty-seven years of statehood.

Just 100 years earlier, Native Americans, mostly Osage and Kansa peoples, had roamed the area hunting and occasionally encountered French and Spanish traders. The only other living things west of the Verdigris River in southeastern Kansas were deer, quail, prairie chickens, and other wildlife.

In 1879, the Frisco Railroad reached Fredonia, which sits atop an ancient bog containing rich veins of coal. By 1918, Jessie's hometown had become a progressive community. In Fredonia's stores, shoppers could buy ginger ale, galvanized iron, ammunition, the latest medicines, coffee pots, dentists' tools, and all sorts of other essential goods.

Opposite: Scott Lake

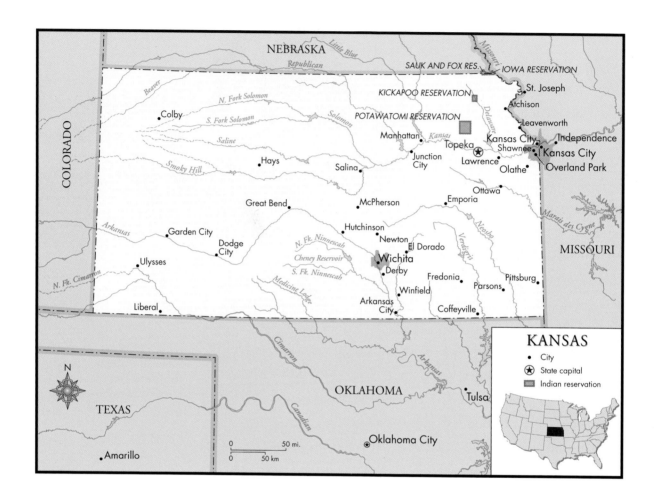

Geopolitical map of Kansas

Jessie loved her hometown, but she wanted to help win the Great War that was raging in Europe. More than 2 million U.S. soldiers were serving in this "war to end all wars," as it was headlined in the Kansas newspapers. Thousands of these soldiers, including many young men Jessie knew in Fredonia, had been called to the armed services through a new program known as "selective service" or "the draft." Jessie had volunteered for overseas duty in social services.

Along with the doughnut and coffee she handed to each soldier, Jessie willingly gave the young men a friendly smile and a cheerful word. She was determined not to let the clouds of war destroy her belief in brighter days ahead.

"As long as there is Kansas, there will be sunshine," Jessie told the weary soldiers. One of the men called her the Kansas sunshine girl. The Associated Press news service picked up the story of her efforts to brighten morale, and Jessie's picture and articles about her spread throughout the United States.

William Allen White, the editor of a leading Kansas newspaper, quoted Jessie's encouraging words, "As long as there is Kansas, there will be sunshine" in the *Emporia Gazette*. White added, "And as long as there is sunshine, there will be Kansas."

CHAPTER TWO

From Seawaters to Statehood

illions of years ago, the area now called Kansas was covered by ocean waters at least fifty different times. Each sea laid down another layer of history in fossils and sediments that turned into rock. For much of the last 2 million years, glaciers covered this region. In fact, one of the great ice ages is called the Kansan. Ice from the north reached down into Kansas, where woolly mammoths roamed the forests.

Many fossils have been found in Kansas.

In the late 1800s, northwestern Kansas became a paradise for paleontologists—scientists who study ancient forms of life. Fossil hunters came from all over to see what they could find in the chalky rock that covered much of the area, and many previously unknown species were discovered. Seven of the thirteen fossilized bird species of the North American continent were found in Kansas.

The competition to find and record new fossils was so intense that the search became known as the Kansas Fossil War. Collectors resorted to bribery and even covered up new finds to keep their rivals from discovering them and claiming credit.

Opposite: Monument Rocks in Gove County

In 1894, Charles H.
Sternberg, a famous
dinosaur hunter from
New York, discovered
the nearly complete
skeleton of a huge
elephant he called the
"hairy mammoth."
The fossil bed in the
northeast part of
Lane County also con-
tained more than 150
elephant teeth.
Today, the Sternberg
Memorial Museum
at Fort Hays State
University displays
fossils of prehistoric
clams, fish, and swim-
ming reptiles. ■

In Search of Quivira

The first people to live in what is now Kansas arrived about 15,000 years ago when the woolly mammoths still roamed the land. The ancestors of these people, named Paleo-Indians by scientists, are believed to have traveled to North America from Asia by a land bridge that once connected the continents.

Native Americans lived in the region long before the first Europeans arrived. When Spanish explorers began to come northward from Mexico in the 1500s, Kansas was occupied by the Wichita, Pawnee, Kansa, Osage, and Kiowa Apache people.

The Kansa, or "people of the south wind," for whom the state is named, were an aloof, proud people. The Kansa lived by growing crops and hunting. Agriculture was women's work, while hunting was the task of the men.

In early 1541, Spanish explorer Francisco Vásquez de Coronado was searching for gold on behalf of the king of Spain. Traveling through Texas, hoping to find a legendary rich kingdom known as Quivira, Coronado turned north. He took about thirty men and an

Francisco Vásquez de Coronado sets out for Quivira.

Spanish conquistadores traveled through Kansas.

Indian guide known as the Turk (because he wrapped his head in what looked like a turban). The Turk assured Coronado that Quivira was located between what is now the Arkansas River and the place where the Republican and Smoky Hill Rivers join to form the Kansas River. There he would find houses full of gold and silver.

After Coronado reached this location, which was inhabited by the Wichita Indians, Coronado ordered the Turk killed. This was not because he hadn't found any gold—although he hadn't—but because Coronado believed the Turk had tried to get the Wichita to kill the Spanish explorers.

Coronado returned to Mexico City, a failure in the eyes of the Spanish crown because he had found no gold or silver. He wrote, "I found only prunes and nuts and very sweet grapes and mulberries."

French and Spanish Claims

For more than a century, Kansas was left to the Native Americans. Then, in 1682, René-Robert Cavelier, Sieur de La Salle, traveled down the Mississippi River from Canada and claimed for France all the land drained by that river. France sent several explorers into the region during the following years, but nothing else was done. France gave the area back to Spain in 1763 when the French lost a major war in Europe. Then Spain passed the region back to France in 1800.

Kansas and the lands west of the Mississippi were not unwanted by everyone, however. Three years later, the United States made the Louisiana Purchase. For only $15 million, the United States acquired 828,000 square miles (2,144,520 sq km) of land. The new territory included almost all of what is now Kansas. One small section of the Louisiana Purchase granted to Spain by the United States in 1819 became part of the Republic of Texas. It finally became part of Kansas when Texas joined the Union in 1845.

The Corps of Discovery

In 1803, President Thomas Jefferson led Congress to appropriate $2,500 for the exploration of the newly acquired lands of the Louisiana Purchase. He selected Captain Meriwether Lewis, his secretary and friend, to lead the expedition, called the Corps of Discovery. Lewis, in turn, chose Lieutenant William Clark to accompany him as coleader. The Lewis and Clark party arrived at the mouth of the Kansas River on June 26, 1804. More than two years later they returned to that location with the first reliable information about the vast area spreading west almost to the Pacific Ocean.

Exploration continued after the Lewis and Clark expedition. Lieutenant Zebulon Montgomery Pike crossed Kansas in 1806 on a journey to gain a peace treaty with the Indians. Pike succeeded in persuading some Pawnee Indians to trade their Spanish flag for the U.S. flag. This was the first time the flag of the United States was raised over Kansas territory by Native Americans.

Meriwether Lewis and William Clark

Both Meriwether Lewis (1774–1809) and William Clark (1770–1838) were born into Virginia farming families. They served together on the frontier in 1795, so when Lewis was offered the leadership of the expedition, he already knew Clark's skills. William Clark was the brother of Revolutionary War hero George Rogers Clark.

After the tremendous accomplishments of their Corps of Discovery exploration, Lewis was appointed governor of the Louisiana Territory. While traveling to Washington, D.C., in 1809, he died mysteriously in a tavern near Nashville, Tennessee. No one knows whether he was murdered or committed suicide.

William Clark became the principal Indian agent for the Louisiana Territory. In 1813, he was named governor of the newly formed Missouri Territory. He was later named Superintendent of Indian Affairs at St. Louis, a position he held until shortly before his death. ■

Opening the West

"What do we want with this vast and worthless area?" That was the question asked by Massachusetts congressman Daniel Webster in 1824. Most of the country's leaders believed the region that included modern Kansas was only a place to pass through on the way to somewhere else.

In 1830 and 1834, Congress passed legislation allowing the U.S. government to use large sections of eastern Kansas as a place to resettle Indians from east of the Mississippi River. White settlers were forbidden to enter Kansas—but not for long.

Along the Santa Fe Trail

William Becknell, a Missouri trader, and a group of about twenty men left Franklin, Missouri, in 1822 with mules loaded with merchandise. They headed for Santa Fe, the Mexican provincial

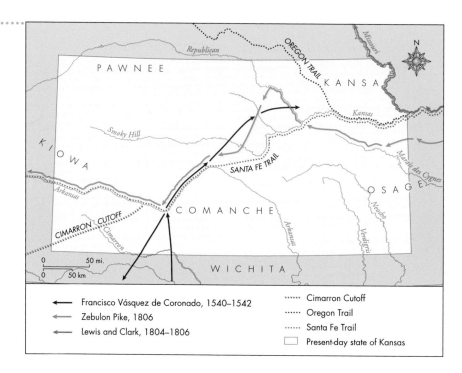

Exploration of Kansas

capital, about 800 miles (1,287 km) away, where they intended to trade. Although the route they took was first traveled in 1792 by explorer Pedro Vial, Becknell is known as the person who established the Santa Fe Trail.

Soon, thousands of wagons traveled this route, which went west from Council Grove along the north bank of the Arkansas River. Those willing to risk extra dangers and hardships took a shorter route, known as the Cimarron Cutoff. They crossed the river near present-day Dodge City and went directly into the waterless sand hills of southwest Kansas. The ruts left by their wagons can still be seen.

It quickly became clear that the Santa Fe Trail was going to become an important highway to the Southwest. The U.S. government signed a treaty with the Osage in 1825 under an oak tree at Council Grove. The treaty officially established the Santa Fe Trail as a public highway. Council Grove itself has been named a national historic landmark.

Along the Oregon Trail

By 1843, westbound pioneers entered Kansas from Missouri, traveled 40 miles (64 km) along the Santa Fe Trail, and then turned their wagons northwest on the route that became the Oregon Trail. The passage of an estimated 300,000 pioneers on the Oregon Trail, called the Great Medicine Road of the Whites by the Indians, is said to be one of the largest voluntary, peacetime mass migrations in human history.

The Oregon Trail became thoroughly worn into the ground of the Great Plains after gold was discovered in California in 1848. Travelers came by the thousands, not only *through* Kansas, but *into*

Travelers along the Oregon Trail

The Wagon Trains

The heavily loaded wagons that carried a family's goods to the West were usually pulled by oxen. According to one pioneer, "One ox is able to pull as much as two mules, does not run off, is easily driven through mud, and will eat almost anything." The wagons traveled in organized groups for protection. These wagon trains were often 1 mile (1.6 km) long and two to four columns wide. Traveling side by side, the wagons could quickly form a circle if they were attacked by Indians. ■

Packing for Pioneering

An Oregon Trail traveler named Joseph E. Ware wrote a helpful book, *The Emigrant's Guide to California.* It provided the following instructions for wagon-train travelers: "Four people in one wagon will need to take 824 pounds of flour, 725 pounds of bacon, 75 pounds of coffee, 160 pounds of sugar, 200 pounds of beans, 200 pounds of lard, 135 pounds of peaches and apples, plus salt and pepper for the four-to-five-month journey." ■

Kansas. By 1850, whites were moving in, ignoring the treaties that had kept settlers out.

Border Wars and Bleeding Kansas

As more and more people settled in the area, Illinois senator Stephen Douglas introduced a bill in Congress creating the two new territories of Kansas and Nebraska. But this led to a problem. In 1820, Congress had passed the Missouri Compromise, a plan

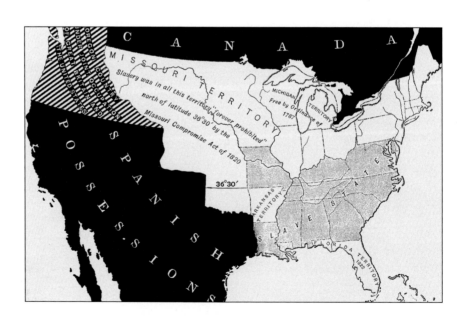

The Missouri Compromise Act

designed to maintain a balance between slave states and free states. The plan banned slavery in any future state north of Missouri's southern border, but many residents of Kansas wanted to own slaves.

Congress repealed, or canceled, the Missouri Compromise with the new Kansas-Nebraska Act of 1854. The new act gave the citizens of each new territory the right to decide whether they would enter the Union as a slave state or a free state. The slavery issue, which had been simmering in the background for several decades, began to erupt again.

Citizens from the Southern states wanted to extend slavery into the new Kansas Territory. The people in the Northern states were equally determined to stop the spread of slavery. These opposing viewpoints quickly led to physical fights and even to murder as the two sides battled to gain control of the territorial government. This sad period of conflict earned the region a nickname—Bleeding Kansas.

Elections for the first Kansas territorial legislature were held on March 30, 1855. On election day, several thousand proslavery men, known as Border Ruffians, crossed into Kansas from Missouri. They stuffed ballot boxes, bullied voters, and intimidated election judges. They helped to defeat the antislavery faction and promptly elected a proslavery bogus legislature, which wrote a strong proslavery constitution. However, Congress had to approve any new territorial constitution, and they rejected the one from the bogus legislature.

Antislavery settlers established the Free State Party. They held their own convention at Topeka in October to draw up a state constitution banning slavery. The following year they elected their own

Stephen Douglas

Jayhawkers

Antislavery supporters known as Free Staters were also called Jayhawkers. A jayhawk is a mythical, plundering bird, half-hawk and half-bluejay. The Free Staters acquired their nickname by crossing the border into Missouri, where they tried to free slaves and plunder the homes of slave owners. The University of Kansas sports teams are still called Jayhawks. ■

governor and legislature. This attempt at governing was also rejected by Congress.

The Pottawatomie Massacre

On May 21, 1856, border ruffians attacked the town of Lawrence, which had been founded by antislavery settlers. Much of the town was burned to ashes. Three days later, antislavery abolitionist John Brown and seven followers—mainly his sons—took personal revenge for the attack because Brown said God had told him to take action. They dragged five proslavery settlers from their cabins along Pottawatomie Creek (about 30 miles [48 km] south of today's Kansas City) and hacked them to death with swords. When a proslavery militia tried to avenge the massacre, Brown and his small group captured the men. Brown became a hero to many Free Staters.

Lawrence after attack by slavery advocates

John Brown

John Brown (1800–1859) spent his earliest years in northwestern Connecticut before moving to Ohio. As a boy, he drove cattle to Detroit to sell to American troops fighting the War of 1812. During that journey, Brown watched a black slave boy being beaten with an iron shovel by his owner. He was so shocked at the sight that he vowed to become slavery's most determined foe.

Though some considered John Brown a hero, his actions at Pottawatomie Creek branded him as a fanatical murderer to many. He fled from Kansas and, with the backing of wealthy Northerners, led an unsuccessful raid on the federal arsenal at Harpers Ferry, Virginia. Convicted of treason, Brown was hanged in 1859.

"John Brown's Body" became one of the most popular Union songs during the Civil War. Brown was also the subject of an epic poem written in 1928 by Stephen Vincent Benét. ■

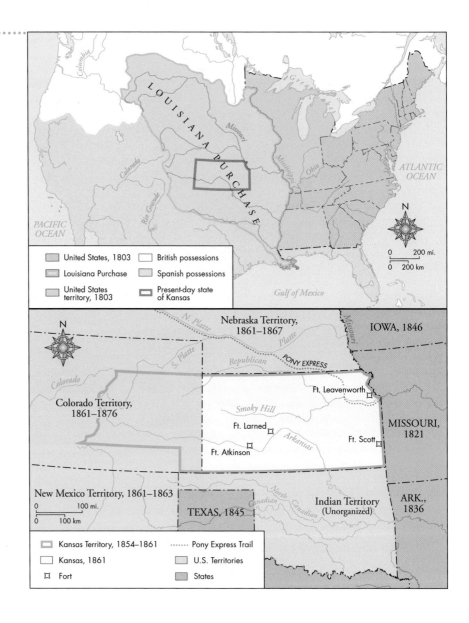

Historical maps
of Kansas

Galloping News of Statehood

Open warfare existed in the Kansas Territory from 1856 to 1858. Three attempts to draw up a state constitution failed to win approval by voters. Finally, in July 1859, a new state constitution prohibiting slavery was drawn up in a convention at Wyandotte,

The Pony Express

now part of Kansas City, Kansas. Voters approved the new constitution the following October, and Congress also approved it. On January 29, 1861, Kansas became the thirty-fourth state in the Union with Topeka as the state capital.

Within days, something unbelievable happened. Half a continent away, people in California celebrated the admittance of Kansas to the Union! Pony Express riders carrying the news had covered 1,966 miles (3,163 km) of wilderness from St. Joseph, Missouri, to San Francisco, California, in only ten days.

The previous year, on April 3, 1860, the first Pony Express rider left St. Joseph. Johnny Fry carried ninety-four letters (at a cost of $5 each), several newspapers, and five telegrams. Less than ten days later, William Hamilton, the last of the thirty westbound relay riders, clattered into Sacramento. Cheers, flags, and marching bands welcomed him. But only ten months after Californians celebrated the news of Kansas statehood, the last Pony Express rider delivered a shipment of mail to San Francisco. This time there were no cheers or marching bands—the Pony Express had been put out of business by the new transcontinental telegraph.

Orphans Preferred

More than 200 applicants answered advertisements soliciting young men eighteen to twenty years of age who weighed "no more than 125 pounds" and were "loyal and fearless." Each rider was required to travel 75 to 100 miles (121 to 161 km) without stopping except to change horses at relay stations. The job paid $50 a month plus room and board. The ads stated, "orphans preferred." ■

Drought and Determination

For two years before statehood, Kansas suffered a devastating drought. Relentless winds and blazing sunshine destroyed crops and dried up rivers. Many settlers left in despair.

Despite the calamities, forty counties had been established in eastern Kansas by 1861. Weekly stagecoach and Pony Express mail schedules linked the territory with the Pacific Coast, while steamboats on the Missouri and Kansas Rivers connected it with the East. The state had more than twenty newspapers, numerous churches, and a school system.

One of the many steamboats that paddled down the Missouri River

On February 12, 1861, President-elect Abraham Lincoln raised a U.S. flag that had, for the first time, a thirty-fourth star—representing Kansas. Lincoln said, "Each additional star has added prosperity and happiness to this country."

The people of Kansas were ready for prosperity and happiness. Unfortunately, the dark days of Bleeding Kansas were far from being over.

CHAPTER THREE

Pioneers and Populism

"**V**olunteers needed to defend the Union!" Kansans eagerly responded to President Lincoln's call for volunteers on April 15, 1861, though Kansas had been a state for only three months and was still recovering from the ravages of drought and territorial warfare. Immediately, 650 Kansas men volunteered for duty. By the time the American Civil War ended in 1865, 20,097 men from Kansas had served in the Union army. That number represented two-thirds of the adult men in the state.

Bushwackers often attacked Union posts in Kansas.

Sacrifice and Glory

Kansas's primary job during the Civil War was to keep the nation's trail system open for supplies and troops from the North. This was an especially tough assignment with Indian conflicts in the remote areas and bandit warfare along the Missouri border. Bandit bands, often called bushwhackers, were continually burning, pillaging, and murdering.

The only major army of the Confederate forces to enter Kansas arrived in the fall of 1864. They were turned back into Missouri at the Battle of Mine Creek in Linn County on October 25. Although no other battles were fought on Kansas ground, Kansas lost more men in the Civil War in proportion to its population than any other state.

Opposite: A sod home in Kansas

Quantrill's Raiders

William Clarke Quantrill (1837–1865) was born in Ohio. He became a teacher, but was restless and kept moving west. In Kansas, he formed a band of about a dozen proslavery men who came to be called Quantrill's Raiders. Union forces called him an outlaw. The Confederacy made him a captain.

On August 21, 1863, Quantrill led 450 bushwhackers into the town of Lawrence. The raiders killed 180 residents and burned most of the town. Union supporters retaliated by looting and burning in four Missouri border counties. Quantrill and his raiders fled to Texas. He was eventually killed during a raid into Kentucky. ■

The Plan That Didn't Work

Under the Homestead Act of 1862, a settler could own a section of land by paying a very small fee and living on the land for five years. Such easy land ownership was heavily promoted after the Civil War as a reward for soldiers, but the plan was flawed from the start. The amount of land designated was 160 acres (65 ha). This was adequate for supporting a family in the well-watered East, but a farmer in Kansas needed at least twice that much land to support a family. As a result, settlers who failed at homesteading sold their land cheap to land speculators and railroads, who later sold it at great profit.

These problems didn't stop homesteaders from coming, though. The decades after the Civil War brought the most intense period of

Buffalo Soldiers

The success of Kansas's First Colored Regiment during the Civil War played a major role in Congress's decision in 1866 to create all-black regiments to serve in the peacetime armies of the United States on the frontier. Organized at Fort Leavenworth, these regiments were called Buffalo Soldiers by the Indians for their fighting spirit and their curly hair. It was a term of respect and honor. ■

settlement in the history of Kansas. Between 1860 and 1890 the population increased from about 100,000 people to 1.4 million. The population growth between 1870 and 1890 exceeded the growth rate for the next eighty years.

Railroads now ran through hunting lands that had been promised to the Native Americans. By 1880, some 200 railroad companies had laid 3,104 miles (4,995 km) of track in Kansas. The railroads lured thousands of people to western Kansas, knowing that the more settlers there were, the more business there would be for the railroads. The Atchison, Topeka and Santa Fe Railroad became one of the largest railroads in the United States. It was chartered in 1859 in Kansas by Cyrus K. Holliday as the Atchison and Topeka Railroad Company. By 1872, it stretched completely across Kansas and along the Santa Fe Trail.

Life in Western Kansas

The lack of wood on the High Plains forced settlers to build homes of sod—hardened dirt and grass. These settlers became known as sodbusters. Sherman Peter Young's parents were typical of the

Wash Day Recipe

"Wash day is the day I detest above all others," wrote a Kansas sodbuster's wife. In spite of her poor spelling, her recipe for doing the family laundry clearly explains why:

1. Bild fire to het kettle of water.
2. Set tubs so smoke won't blow in eyes if wind is pert.
3. Shave hole cake lie sope in bilin water.
4. Make piles. 1 pile white, 1 pile cullord, 1 pile work briches and rags.
5. Stur flour in cold water to smooth, then thin down with bilin water for starch.
6. Rub dirty spots on board. Scrub hard, then bile.
7. Take white things out of kettle with broom stick. Then rench, blew and starch.
8. Turn tub upside down after pouring rench water in flower bed and scrubbing porch with soapy water.

(From *Pioneer Women Voices from the Kansas Frontier* by Joanna L. Stratton)

sodbusters who hoped for a better life in Kansas. Their determination was severely tested in 1874 when, on the heels of a drought, a plague of grasshoppers invaded the state. "They came in great hordes, forming clouds that darkened the sky," Young recalled of his early childhood on the Kansas plains. "They ate my father's entire peach crop, leaving only the bare stones hanging on bare trees."

The First Female Dentist

Lucy Hobbs Taylor (1833–1910) came to Kansas in 1867, but not to be a prairie housewife. The New York–born woman wanted to be a dentist, but no school would admit a female. She persuaded a dentist in Cincinnati to let her be an apprentice and thus she learned her work. Only after she was already working as a dentist did a school—the Ohio College of Dental Surgery—grant her a degree. So Lucy Hobbs Taylor, the world's first academically qualified woman dentist, also became the first woman dentist to work in Kansas. She and her husband ran their practice in Lawrence for many years. ▪

Even without grasshoppers, life was hard. A Kansas prairie housewife put in long hours cooking, cleaning, sewing, gardening, and laundering. She had to get the family's daily water supply, sometimes trudging 1 mile (1.6 km) or more to the nearest running stream. Gathering the family's fuel supply meant searching the prairie for twigs, weeds, and dried dung from grazing cattle and buffalo. The dried dung was stored in a sack to provide fuel for heating and cooking in the winter.

Cavalry and Cowboys

The U.S. military built a number of forts in Kansas. The forts were intended to maintain peace among Native American peoples and to protect both the settlers and railroads. However, the U.S. government often failed to protect the Indians' territorial rights and to uphold treaties. The Native American peoples became increasingly frustrated with treaty violations and with settlers taking over their lands. From 1865 to 1869, hostile encounters between the settlers and Indians increased dramatically.

As the army expanded its system of forts in Kansas, businessmen, such as Joseph G. McCoy, saw the opportunity to sell herds

Military Forts in Kansas

1827 Colonel Henry Leavenworth establishes Fort Leavenworth, the first permanent white settlement in what would become Kansas. Today it is used as a federal prison (above).

1842 The U.S. Army establishes Fort Scott. Today it commemorates events of the Civil War.

1859 The U.S. Army establishes Camp Alert. This post is later moved and renamed Fort Larned.

1864 Fort Ellsworth is established. This fort is later moved and renamed Fort Harker.

1865 Fort Hays, Fort Dodge, and Fort Wallace are established.

of Texas longhorn cattle to the military. McCoy arrived in Abilene in 1867 with a herd of cattle he had driven up a trail established by Jesse Chisholm. That same year, the first railroad line in central Kansas—the Union Pacific, Eastern Division—reached Abilene. McCoy built corrals and established Abilene as the first actual "cow town" of Kansas.

Over the next five years, 3 million head of cattle moved up the Chisholm Trail to Abilene. A typical herd of 2,500 animals was moved by a dozen cowboys. In Abilene, as many as 5,000 cowboys were often paid on the day after they had spent three months driving cattle. The lawmen who were hired to keep the peace in Abilene became the stuff of Wild West legend.

Legendary Lawmen

"Bear River" Tom Smith (1830–1870) was hired as the marshal of Abilene in 1870. The fearless Smith had earned his nickname in Wyoming, where he had also been a marshal. He was the first law officer to keep the rowdies from drawing their six-shooters in Abilene. He was killed while trying to arrest a homesteader. His death marked the return of lawlessness to Abilene until the following year, when "Wild Bill" Hickok took the job of marshal.

James Butler "Wild Bill" Hickok (1837–1876) (above) was born in Illinois. A stagecoach driver, guerrilla fighter, and scout for General George Custer, Hickok achieved fame as a U.S. marshal in Abilene. His success

in Abilene drew large audiences when he later toured with "Buffalo Bill" Cody's Wild West Show, astonishing audiences with his precise marksmanship. Hickok was shot and killed from behind by a stranger while playing poker in a saloon in Deadwood, Dakota Territory.

Wyatt Earp (1848–1929) (right), also from Illinois, worked first as a police officer in Wichita. For several years on and off he served as a deputy marshal in Dodge City, but he never stayed long. He finally left for Tombstone, Arizona, where he furthered his reputation for being fearless. He and his brother Virgil became unpopular after shooting three troublemaking cowboys at the OK Corral. They outlived the Wild West. ▧

A cattle drive from Texas to Kansas

The rough-and-ready cowtowns of the West couldn't last. The Texas cattle carried ticks. They were immune to the fever caused by the ticks, but other cattle were not. The Kansas Quarantine Laws of 1884 and 1885 put an end to cattle from Texas being driven through the state. The period of the cattle drives, cattle drovers, and legendary lawmen was short-lived, but much of Kansas today is built upon the legacy it left behind.

Stopping the Wind

During the Civil War, Congress had authorized President Lincoln to proceed with the extinction of all Indian land titles in Kansas. The government wanted to move all eastern Indians to Oklahoma, which was then called Indian Territory. Congress thought that if the army eliminated the buffalo, or bison, which provided the native peoples with food and other necessities of life, the Indians would be forced out of Kansas.

The railroad companies, anxious to move the rails of the "iron horse" farther west, also called for the destruction of the buffalo. William "Buffalo Bill" Cody was said to have killed 4,280 buffalo in the eighteen months he worked for the Kansas Pacific Railroad.

Employees of the railroad killing buffalo

Bison Facts

- An estimated 20 million bison (or American buffalo) roamed the western plains in 1850. Millions were killed in the later part of the century.
- Hide from the neck of the bison was used to make shields. It was so tough it repelled bullets.
- There are no known allergies to the hair, flesh, or blood of the bison.
- Bison can run at speeds of 35 miles (56 km) per hour.
- About 100,000 buffalo lived in the U.S. in private herds and protected areas in 1998.

In 1867, about 15,000 Indians from five tribes gathered at Medicine Lodge to discuss peace with representatives of the U.S. government. They agreed to surrender all lands north of the Arkansas River if they could keep the rest of the lands that had previously been promised to them "forever." Comanche chief Ten Bears pleaded, "I was born on the prairie where the wind blew free

Father of the Exodus

Benjamin "Pap" Singleton (1809–1892) was born in Nashville, Tennessee. He was sold several times as a slave before he escaped to Michigan. Singleton was convinced it was his mission to help his people improve their lives. After the slaves were freed in 1863, he formed a company that helped hundreds of former slaves move to Kansas. Singleton is known as the Father of the Exodus. ∎

and there was nothing to break the light of the sun. I want to die there and not within walls." But no one listened. A decade later, the buffalo herds had been destroyed, and almost all Native Americans had been removed from Kansas.

Four groups of Native American peoples have lands in Kansas today. Brown County has the Kickapoo Reservation near Horton, the Iowa Reservation near Hiawatha, and the Sauk and Fox Reservation near Reserve and White Cloud. The Potawatomi Reservation is in Jackson County near Mayetta.

The Exodusters

After the Civil War, freed slaves began to trickle into Kansas. Soon, the trickle became a tide. More than 20,000 freed slaves settled in Kansas between 1870 and 1880. African-Americans were known as Exodusters—a nickname taken from the word *exodus*, meaning the movement of large numbers of people out of an area. The Exodusters settled primarily in three communities—Dunlap, Singleton, and Nicodemus.

At first, Kansas welcomed the Exodusters. Then, as more and more arrived, they were no longer welcomed. About two-thirds of the Exodusters left the state when the railroads bypassed their towns and when they realized that farming in the Great Plains was very different from growing cotton in the South.

In 1967, the U.S. Department of the Interior designated the community of Nicodemus as a national historic landmark. Each year the town hosts the Emancipation Celebration, known as Homecoming, a reunion for descendants of the Exodusters.

Dry Kansas

The sale of liquor to Indians was prohibited in Kansas in 1860. Many counties and towns prohibited the sale of all liquor, but it was not until 1881 that the state prohibition law was passed. That law prohibited the manufacture and sale of intoxicating beverages "except for medicinal or scientific purposes."

Then in 1919, the entire nation instituted the Eighteenth Amendment to the Constitution in response to the many temperance movements around the country that wanted to abolish alcohol. This amendment prohibited the manufacture, sale, and transportation of alcoholic beverages in the United States. The amendment was repealed in 1933 by the Twenty-First Amendment, when citizens realized that Prohibition caused more crime and misery than it stopped.

A prohibition camp meeting at Bismark Grove

The Woman with a Hatchet

Carry A. Nation (1846–1911) launched a career of saloon-smashing and temperance crusades in Medicine Lodge in 1890. Years of abuse because of her first husband's alcoholism led her to despise liquor, and she wanted to be sure that Kansas's drinking laws were enforced.

Nation published a newsletter, *Smasher's Mail*, which identified judges who ignored prohibition laws. On January 21, 1901, she began using a hatchet to smash up saloons. She later sold tiny hatchets to raise money for her temperance efforts and to pay her many fines. ▧

A Grange meeting

Popular Populism

Droughts and grasshoppers were only two of the many obstacles Kansas farmers had to contend with during the late 1800s. As one farmer put it, constant battles against unregulated control by banks and railroads "went right along with battling blizzards and bugs."

A group of Kansas farmers began a local Society of Patrons of Husbandry, which became known as the Grange movement. The Grangers' goals were to fight the high prices that railroads charged for carrying grain and to improve farm life.

Other farm and labor parties also became active. The Kansas Farmers' Alliance joined with the Grangers, Single Tax Club, Industrial Union, Knights of Labor, and other groups of working-class citizens to form the People's, or Populist, Party. The Populists' goals centered on the belief that the working class had been

The End of the Wild West

Emmett Dalton (1871–1937), along with his two brothers and other gang members, tried to rob two banks in Coffeyville on October 5, 1892. However, the citizens of Coffeyville surprised the Dalton Gang by fighting back. Emmett was the only Dalton to survive. Four citizens who had taken part in the gunfight were also killed. Though sentenced to life in prison, Dalton was released in 1907 with a full pardon from the governor. He became a model citizen, giving lectures across the country on behalf of law and order. At a speech in Coffeyville in 1931, he said, "The biggest fool on earth is the one who thinks crime can be made to pay." ▪

neglected by the government and taken advantage of by big business.

The Kansas Populists' most powerful spokesman was a cattleman who had been ruined by the devastating blizzard of 1886. Jeremiah Simpson gained the nickname Sockless Jerry after a speech he made about the plight of the poor working man who couldn't even afford socks. The Populists won the governorship of Kansas in 1892, electing Lorenzo D. Lewelling, and served as an example to People's Parties all over the country.

A battle during the siege of San Juan, Puerto Rico, in the Spanish-American War

Bleeding Kansas Bleeds Again

Spain's refusal to grant independence to Cuba, and the sinking of the U.S. battleship *Maine* in the harbor of Havana, Cuba, brought the United States into a war against Spain in 1898. The 850 members of the Kansas Twenty-Third Colored Regiment were the first American soldiers to leave U.S. soil to fight the war. The all-black Tenth U.S. Cavalry was among the U.S. forces to charge up Kettle Hill on July 1, 1898.

As the 1800s ended, such Kansas newspapers as the *Emporia Gazette* reported that "an era of good feeling" prevailed in the state. Kansans began turning their attention from the battlefields to the beginning of a new century.

CHAPTER FOUR

Mileposts to the Future

Kansas moved toward the twentieth century with its feet firmly planted in the soil and its eyes focused on the future. Primarily a corn-growing state, Kansas was about to become the world's leading wheat-producing region.

Immigrants from southern Russia had arrived in Kansas in 1874 bringing with them hardy, drought-resistant "Turkey red" wheat to plant. "Turkey Red Puts Kansas in the Black" read the headlines of the state's newspapers as the new century began.

Nineteenth-century farmers plowing the Kansas prairie

First Steps

Kansas lawmakers soon made life better for many people. Workers enjoyed an eight-hour workday. A board of commissioners curbed the power of the railroads, and legislation regulated the oil industry. The legislature also established compulsory education, a textbook commission, and pensions for indigent mothers.

Science and technology were changing Kansas from a remote prairie to a modern state. The first telephone rang in Kansas in 1877. The first wire to bring electricity to rural areas was strung between Atchison and Tonganoxie in 1910. The smell of Mentholatum, known as "the little nurse in a bottle," filled the air in Wichita, where Albert Hyde had invented the popular medicinal rub.

Opposite: Migrant workers heading west during the Great Depression

A Model T Ford

Mass-produced Model T automobiles rumbled into Kansas in 1908. Henry Ford built his first tractor that same year. Horses were still the most common means of transportation in 1910 when Jessie Spencer, who would later serve coffee and doughnuts to soldiers in France, traveled from Fredonia to Wichita. She came to watch a daring exhibition of a flying machine by pilot Ruth Law. Most people were content to stay on the ground—the State Highway Commission claimed their 2,500 miles (4,022 km) of roads were "safe at 25 mph [40 kph] during 10 months out of the year."

Winning the Great War

President Woodrow Wilson's announcement in 1914 that the United States would remain neutral in the war in Europe was welcomed by Kansans. Oil discoveries had brought boom days to the state. Salt deposits had been discovered under most of central and western Kansas, and salt-mining operations were underway. For the first year ever, the number of acres of wheat planted exceeded the number of acres of corn planted. Kansans did not think a war happening so far away could affect them.

But the interception of a secret message by the British government in February 1917 changed Kansans from favoring neutrality to calling for war against Germany. The message, which was shown to President Woodrow Wilson, contained a convincing offer by Germany to Mexico: If Mexico would help Germany win the war in Europe, Germany would return Texas, New Mexico, and Arizona to Mexico. The citizens of Kansas were alarmed because the southwestern corner of Kansas had once been part of Texas.

On April 6, 1917, the United States declared war on Germany. Kansas again furnished more than its share of soldiers. Kansas farmers also contributed greatly to the Allied victory by rallying to the cry "Win the War with Wheat!" They produced millions of bushels of wheat—not only to feed the soldiers but also to feed the starving people of war-torn Europe.

Camp Funston, established in 1917 on Pawnee Flats and named for Spanish-American War hero Frederick Funston of Kansas, was one of the largest military training centers in the nation. Fort Leavenworth was also an important training center.

A military brigade standing in banner formation at Camp Funston

Swat the Fly!

Samuel Crumbine (1862–1954) helped Kansas become a leader in the field of public health. From 1904 to 1920, he served as secretary of the state board of health. During that time, he crusaded against the fraudulent labeling of drugs, improper handling of food, contaminated water, and sharing drinking cups. His "Swat the Fly" and "Don't Spit on the Sidewalk" slogans won national recognition. ■

At the Kansas Oil
Museum in El Dorado

Roaring Kansas

The 1920s opened with a U.S. population of almost 106 million. For the first time since 1790, when the Constitution required a census to be taken every ten years, the population of rural America dropped to less than 50 percent of the total population. The number of farm residents had dwindled to less than 30 percent.

New mineral discoveries had Kansans digging deeper than any plow to harvest what lay beneath Kansas soil. On July 20, 1920, natural gas was discovered near Liberal. The Hugoton Field, which lies under much of southwestern Kansas, is one of the largest natural gas fields in the world. Though discovered only five years earlier, the El Dorado Oil Field in Butler County was producing more than 29 million barrels of oil a year. Enormous deposits of coal in southeastern Kansas were also being mined. Half of the nation's zinc was being smelted (separated from its ore) in Pittsburg. This made zinc the largest nonfood industry in the state.

Ku Klux Klan in Kansas

An organization dedicated to hate arrived in Kansas in 1923. Members of the Ku Klux Klan (KKK) marched in the streets wearing hoods and white sheets. They were anti-Jewish, anti-Catholic, and anti-black. William Allen White, editor of the *Emporia Gazette,* won a Pulitzer Prize for his editorials against the KKK. He wrote, "It is an organization of cowards. It is a menace to peace and decent neighborly living." White campaigned against the KKK by running for governor as an independent candidate in 1924. He lost the election, but in 1925 the state refused to issue the KKK a charter, and the organization faded in Kansas. ■

The Bad Years

The crash of the stock market in New York in 1929 sent the United States into an economic slump known as the Great Depression. Kansas suffered enormous financial setbacks that threatened to wipe out all of its gains. From locomotive shops in Topeka to flour mills on the western plains, business and industry in Kansas ground to a halt.

Dust storms between 1932 and 1939 earned Kansas the grim title of the Dust Bowl State. Too many years of too little rain, plus too many acres of grasslands now used as wheat fields, had turned the soil to powder. Thousands of farmers abandoned their land as "black blizzards" turned noonday skies dark with blowing dirt. Livestock suffocated to death. Some people died of acute respiratory infections.

Franklin Delano Roosevelt became the thirty-second U.S. president in 1933. His New Deal program to bring the nation out of the depression established numerous farm-service agencies and programs designed to help the country's agriculture and livestock production.

By the time rain fell on Kansas in 1939, the federal and state governments had started conservation programs to help

The Kansas Dust Bowl in the 1930s

Kansas recover from the depression and the drought. These included soil conservation and crop diversification. In addition, public works projects provided money to build public buildings and roads, and to fund arts programs that put people to work and improved the quality of life.

Building Bombers in the Breadbasket

World War II (1939–1945) dominated the 1940s in Kansas. After Japan attacked Pearl Harbor in Hawaii on December 7, 1941, Kansans once again rushed to volunteer for military service.

When the war began, Kansas was already an established manufacturing center for cars and farm equipment. Plants such as General Motors and International Harvester were converted to produce aircraft. Boeing Company in Wichita built 1,600 B-29 Superfortresses, the largest airplanes built in the United States during World War II. Munitions plants and hundreds of other war-supply manufacturing facilities spread across Kansas.

American air power turned the tide of the war in both Europe and the Pacific. The Allies were able to push the advancing Japanese back. However, Japan refused to surrender. Japanese leaders vowed to con-

A B-29 during World War II

tinue the fighting even if it meant the death of millions of their own people. On August 6, 1945, after repeated warnings, the United States dropped an atomic bomb on the city of Hiroshima in Japan from a B-29 aircraft named the *Enola Gay.* Japan still refused to surrender, and another atomic bomb was dropped on the city of Nagasaki on August 9. This brought an immediate end to the war.

The Impact of the Fifties

The "dirty thirties" returned to Kansas as the "filthy fifties" with yet another drought. The driest five years in the state's history occurred from 1952 to 1957.

Two other events during the 1950s would have far-reaching impacts. The first was the 1952 election of General Dwight D. Eisenhower as the nation's thirty-fourth president. Eisenhower, who grew up in Abilene, Kansas, had become famous as the supreme commander of Allied forces in Europe during World War II.

The second event occurred in 1954. That year the U.S. Supreme Court heard the case of *Brown* v. *Board of Education of Topeka.* The father of an eleven-year-old black girl named Linda Brown sued the Topeka Board of Education for not allowing his daughter to attend an all-white school. The Court ruled unanimously that it was unconstitutional for public schools to be segregated by race. This historic decision resulted in the gradual desegregation of public schools across the United States.

Kansas's Contribution to the Air War (percentage of planes built in U.S.)

Transport gliders	18%
Transport aircraft	23%
Trainer aircraft	27%
Medium bombers	31%
Heavy bombers	41%

Thurgood Marshall (center) along with attorneys George E. C. Hayes (left) and James Nabrit Jr. after winning *Brown* v. *Board of Education of Topeka*

Turbulent Times

In his farewell address to the nation on January 17, 1961, President Eisenhower said, "America's leadership and prestige depend on how we use our power in the interests of world peace and human betterment." The turbulent years of the 1960s saw Kansans serving in both the Peace Corps and the Vietnam War. Some students at Kansas's universities protested U.S. involvement in Vietnam through demonstrations. Others saw the war as an opportunity to demonstrate their patriotism. "Kansans are individualists today as much as they were a hundred years ago," noted then-U.S. representative Robert Dole of Kansas.

In the early 1970s, severe drought hit the state again. Scientists say the Kansas climate pattern has become fairly predictable. They say Kansas can expect to suffer from a major drought every twenty years or so.

"Kansas was saved in 1972 by Russia's purchase of millions of bushels of Kansas wheat. At the same time, it lost thousands of acres to serious soil erosion," says author David Worster. "It is still nature that gives and nature that takes away."

Kansans have been concerned with other issues, too. Child abuse, battered women, and drug dependency are social problems in rural as well as urban communities. In 1980, Kansas became the first state to create a fund for child-abuse-prevention programs.

To the Stars

In the 1980s and 1990s, Kansas was as much about satellites and pizza as it was about cattle and wheat. Kansans were piloting spacecraft and helping develop new technologies for exploring

Pizza Hut

On June 15, 1958, brothers Dan and Frank Carney borrowed $600 from their mother and opened the first Pizza Hut restaurant in a small rented building in Wichita. Ten years later, the number of Pizza Hut restaurants had reached 300 and Pizza Hut had branched into Canada. In 1977, the chain merged with PepsiCo, and by 1995, there were more than 10,000 Pizza Huts around the world. ■

the solar system as well as providing opportunities for individuals to launch personal business ventures.

New manufacturing plants continue to be built in Kansas. Many insurance and communication companies have large corporate headquarters in Kansas. The aviation industry now contributes more to the economy of Kansas than wheat does. Kansans are still more likely, however, to talk about wheat and cattle prices than about aircraft.

In 1998, Governor Bill Graves summarized Kansas's role in the global economy: "The world is consuming Kansas-grown grain and meat, flying Kansas-built aircraft, and using Kansas-built machinery, while Kansas-based services meet their needs. Kansas has positioned itself to step into the future. Kansas will be ready when the future arrives."

CHAPTER FIVE

The Nature of Kansas

The word *Kansa* probably first appeared on a map drawn in 1673 by Father Jacques Marquette, a French missionary. *Kansa* is an Indian word meaning "people of the south wind." Kansas is the fourth-windiest state in the United States after Massachusetts, Montana, and Wyoming.

Other early maps, like those drawn by explorer Zebulon Pike in 1806 and Major Stephen Long in 1819, labeled Kansas and the Great Plains the "Great American Desert." Dr. Charles Robinson's scouting report to the New England Emigrant Aid Society, however, painted a completely different picture: "The prairie seems to be an endless succession of rolls, with a smooth green surface, dotted all over with the most beautiful flowers. The soil is of the most rich and fertile character, with no waste land. The feelings that come over a person as he first views this immense ocean of land are indescribable."

Wind often rolls through the wheat fields in Kansas.

The Lay of the Land

Kansas covers an area of 82,282 square miles (213,110 sq km), making it the fifteenth-largest state. Kansas is bounded on the north by Nebraska, on the east by Missouri, on the south by Oklahoma, and on the west by Colorado. The state stretches 408 miles (656 km) from east to west and 206 miles (331 km) from north to

Opposite: Flint Hills Tallgrass Prairie in Butler County

Bringing the Immigrants

Dr. Charles Robinson (1818–1894) was born in Massachusetts and practiced medicine there before traveling west as an explorer. He returned to Massachusetts where he worked with the New England Emigrant Aid Society. The Society's purpose was to bring immigrants to settle the West. Robinson himself led the second party of immigrants to Kansas, where they settled the town of Lawrence.

Robinson was elected the first governor of Kansas. His wife, Sara, recorded much of the state's history and geography. Her book, *Kansas, Its Interior and Exterior Life*, is credited with encouraging hundreds of immigrants to come to Kansas. ■

south. It is almost a rectangle except for the bite cut out by the Missouri River in the northeastern corner. "It looks like a grilled cheese sandwich with the corner nibbled out," wrote a Colby fourth-grader.

Contrary to popular belief, Kansas is not a flat, featureless plain. The surface climbs from an elevation of 680 feet (207 m) at

Kansas's Geographical Features

Total area; rank	82,282 sq. mi. (213,110 sq km); 14th
Land; rank	81,823 sq. mi. (211,922 sq km); 14th
Water; rank	459 sq. mi. (1,189 sq km); 40th
Inland water; rank	459 sq. mi. (1,189 sq km); 34th
Geographic center	Barton, 15 miles (24 km) northeast of Great Bend
Highest point	Mount Sunflower, 4,039 feet (1,231 m)
Lowest point	Verdigris River, 680 feet (207 m)
Largest city	Wichita
Population; rank	2,485,600 (1990 census); 32nd
Record high temperature	121°F (49°C) at Fredonia on July 18, 1936
Record low temperature	–40°F (–40°C) at Lebanon on February 13, 1905
Average July temperature	78°F (26°C)
Average January temperature	30°F (–1°C)
Average annual precipitation	27 inches (69 cm)

the Verdigris River in Montgomery County in the southeastern corner, to its highest point, 4,039 feet (1,231 m) at Mount Sunflower in Wallace County along the western boundary. A sign at the western edge of Kinsley in Edwards County marks the halfway point between San Francisco and New York.

Geographic Regions

Kansas is divided into four main geographic regions. Two of the four regions are part of the Great Plains, which cover the center of the United States. The High Plains, in the western third of the state, is part of the increasingly elevated area leading to the Rocky Mountains. It is practically treeless, but valleys, ravines, and canyons run into the mountains.

The Plains Border region occupies the middle third of the state. This is an area dotted with hills, dunes, chalk beds, and rock formations.

The Southeastern Plains includes the Flint Hills, named for their limestone ridges, and the Osage Plains. These areas are covered by bluestem grasses and rank among the world's best grazing areas.

The Dissected Till Plains area in the northeast corner is a hilly, forested region with many creeks and springs. Its name indicates that the region was once covered by glaciers that cut up, or dissected, the land with many ridges and valleys.

Grass and Flowers

Much of Kansas is prairie, or grassland, and about 200 kinds of grasses grow in the state. Big bluestem— also known as bluejoint

Geographic versus Geodetic Centers

A stone marker pinpoints the geographic center of the forty-eight contiguous states, 1 mile (1.6 km) north of the town of Lebanon. This geographic center should not be confused with the geodetic center of North America, which is also in Kansas and is located about 40 miles (64 km) south of Lebanon.

The geodetic center is marked by a triangle-shaped disk located on a ranch in Osborne County. The dot in the center of the disk is the continent's center, and is used by surveyors in measuring North America. Geodetic measurements include corrections for the curvature of the earth. ■

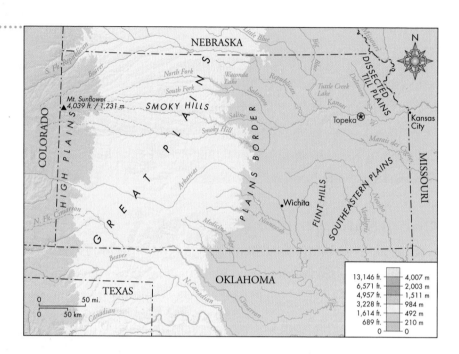

Topographical map of Kansas

turkeyfoot—and little bluestem—known as prairie beardgrass—grow in almost every part of the state. They form the basis of Kansas's enormous livestock industry.

Indian grass, side-oats grama, prairie dropseed, sand dropseed, and sloughgrass are found in eastern Kansas. Buffalo, blue grama, hairy grama, sandreed, and salt grass grow in western Kansas. Tumble grass, green bristle, switchgrass, and western wheatgrass thrive in the north-central section.

The wild sunflower has become the symbol of Kansas. Other Kansas wildflowers include mayapples, Dutchman's-breeches, evening primroses, asters, clovers, columbines, goldenrods, sweet williams, thistles, verbenas, and wild morning glories.

Trees and Forests

The Kansas National Forest was established in 1905 and covered more than 300,000 acres (121,410 ha) of sand hills south of the

Arkansas River. More than 800,000 trees were planted, mostly pine and hardwoods such as locust and Osage orange.

In 1911, a severe drought wiped out nearly all the hardwoods, and the dry conditions of southwest Kansas proved to be too much for the pine trees. On October 14, 1915, President Woodrow Wilson abolished the ten-year-old Kansas National Forest. The northeastern corner of the former forest area, now the Finney Game Refuge, is the home of the oldest publicly owned herd of bison in Kansas.

Bison at the Finney Game Refuge

Tremendous Trees

There is only one tree in the Kansas State Forest in Pottawatomie County. Called the Vieux ("old") Elm, it is almost 300 years old. At more than 99 feet (30.2 m) in height and 23 feet (7 m) around, it is the largest American elm in the world. Its branches span about 133 feet (40.6 m).

The Post Office Oak in Council Grove (in foreground above) is another famous Kansas tree. Westward-bound travelers along the Santa Fe Trail once left letters in its hollow. The American Forestry Association honored the Post Office Oak by naming it to its Hall of Fame for trees. ■

Tallgrass Prairie National Preserve

In 1996, Congress designated the Tallgrass Prairie National Preserve as Kansas's first national park. Former senator Nancy Landon Kassebaum, whose efforts led to the park's establishment, describes the park as "ten thousand acres that contain no towering rocks or dramatic canyons. Only grass, wind, wildlife, sunshine, and a night sky free of city lights." ■

The red cedar found throughout the state is actually a juniper. It is the only coniferous, or cone-bearing, evergreen tree native to Kansas.

Hackberry, oak, willow, black walnut, and sycamore trees grow in eastern Kansas. Box elder and cottonwood predominate in western Kansas, while sassafras trees are found in the southeastern part of the state.

In 1894, only two apple trees bearing fruit were reported in Kansas. Today, the fruit trees of northeastern Kansas produce millions of pounds of apples and peaches each year. Doniphan County produces about one-third of all the apples grown in the state. Annual apple production there averages more than 4 million pounds (1.8 million kg). Sedgwick County leads the state in peach production with nearly half of the commercial peach crop.

Mineral Resources

Kansas ranks among the top ten mineral-producing states in the United States. Petroleum, natural gas, coal, lead, zinc, stone, clay, salt, sand, and gypsum are the leading minerals. Kansas is one of the world's major producers of gypsum, mineral used in drywall building materials.

Some of the deepest oil and gas wells have been drilled in the Hugoton Gas Field underlying southwestern Kansas. Helium is also found in Kansas gas.

Coal mining in Kansas

Limestone was formed millions of years ago from the shells of animals that lived in the ancient seas in the center of what is now North America. Today, limestone from various areas of Kansas is used for many construction purposes, including gravel for roads and highways and buildings such as the state capitol and the Eisenhower Museum. Fence post rock is an interesting form of limestone also used in construction. It can be easily cut and carved when it is fresh out of the ground. Prolonged exposure to air hardens it.

Sand, found in abundance along the path

One of Kansas's many sinkholes

of the Arkansas River, is regularly dug and dredged. The production of sand and gravel is the most widespread nonfuel mineral industry in the state.

Huge salt deposits lie under much of central Kansas. The state produces more than a million tons of salt each year, but this hardly makes a dent in the amount of salt under Kansas. An estimated 13 trillion tons of salt lie under the Hutchinson area alone.

Wetlands and Sinks

The Jamestown State Waterfowl Management Area is a large salt marsh that provides habitat for birds and other wildlife. This salt marsh is one of a series of salt springs, seeps, and marshes in Kansas. The marsh is a stopover for many migrating birds on the central flyway route to Canada.

Sinkholes, or sinks, are funnel-shaped depressions in the land's surface caused by the collapse of the roofs of underground caverns. Some sinkholes are as much as 100 feet (30 m) deep and 1 mile (1.6 km) in diameter. Mining in Kansas is the principal cause of the more than 300 sinkholes in the state.

The marshy swampland of Cheyenne Bottoms Wildlife Area makes up more than 19,000 acres (7,689 ha) of wetlands. It was originally part of a 41,000-acre (16,590-ha) sinkhole. According to the Kansas Fish and Game Commission, more than half of all U.S. migratory waterfowl pass through this wildlife sanctuary in Barton County.

Water, Parks, and Wildlife

Kansas is drained by two main watersheds. The Kansas River and its tributaries flow eastward through the northern half of the state. The Arkansas River and its tributaries flow in a generally southeast direction through the southern part.

A small area is drained by the Marais des Cygnes River, a French name meaning "marsh of swans." This river later becomes the Osage. In the extreme northeast, the streams flow into the Missouri River. Other principal rivers in Kansas are the Big Blue, Republican, Solomon, Saline, Smoky Hill, Cimarron, and Neosho.

Enormous amounts of farm runoff and city wastewater end up in the Kansas River. The Kansas Natural Resource Council and the

Cave Country

The Kansas Speleological Society has cataloged 528 caves in 37 Kansas counties. Comanche County has the largest number, with 128. These caves often shelter large populations of bats. Some of the caves, such as Palmer Cave north of Lake Kanopolis in Ellsworth County, contain ancient Indian petroglyphs, or drawings on stone. ■

Water pollution is still a concern to many Kansans

Kansas Natural Heritage Program are two groups working to improve the condition of the river.

More than 10,000 miles (16,090 km) of Kansas streams are great for fishing. White and largemouth bass, bluegill, crappie, catfish, carp, and walleye are abundant in the state's rivers and lakes. Kansas farmers and ranchers have also built more than 55,000 ponds that they stock with bass, bluegill, and channel catfish.

More than 200 natural lakes and 25 reservoirs (humanmade lakes) punctuate the Kansas plains. Milford Lake, the largest lake in Kansas, was formed by a dam on the Republican River and covers about 16,000 acres (6,475 ha). Other major reservoirs include Cedar Bluff, Cheney, Council Grove, Elk City, Fall River, Glen Elder, John Redmond, Kanopolis, Kirwin, Lovewell, Norton, Perry, Pomona, Toronto, Tuttle Creek, Webster, and Wilson.

Tuttle Creek Lake

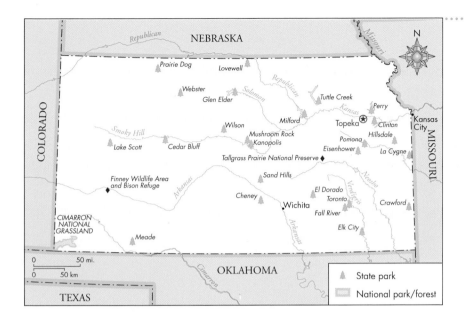

Map labels:

NEBRASKA

Republican

Prairie Dog
Lovewell
Webster
Glen Elder
Solomon
Republican
Tuttle Creek
Perry
Kansas
Wilson
Milford
Topeka ✪
Clinton
Kansas City
Mushroom Rock
Hillsdale
Smoky Hill
Kanopolis
Pomona
Lake Scott
Cedar Bluff
Eisenhower
La Cygne
Tallgrass Prairie National Preserve ◆
Sand Hills
Neosho
Finney Wildlife Area and Bison Refuge ◆
Arkansas
El Dorado
Verdigris
Cheney
Toronto
Crawford
Wichita
Fall River
CIMARRON NATIONAL GRASSLAND
Elk City
Meade

COLORADO

MISSOURI

N

0   50 mi.
0   50 km

Cimarron
OKLAHOMA
TEXAS
Arkansas

▲ State park
▢ National park/forest

**Kansas's parks
and forests**

Along with these reservoirs, there are state parks and a variety of wildlife preserves. These areas support such animals as beaver, raccoon, bobcat, gray fox, mink, muskrat, bobwhite quail, deer, and waterfowl.

Kansas is also home to five subspecies of poisonous snakes, including the rare western cottonmouth water moccasin. Of its thirty amphibian species, Kansas boasts one that weighs more than 130 pounds (59 kg)—the alligator snapping turtle.

Endangered Species

Kansas was known as a hunter's paradise in the 1860s. Shooting parties from as far away as Europe bagged huge numbers of bear, panther, timber wolf, deer, otter, and beaver. Farther west were herds of bison and vast numbers of quail, wild turkey, and other game birds and migratory waterfowl.

By 1925, the bear, wolf, panther, grouse (prairie chicken), and wild turkey had been almost totally eliminated from Kansas. Quail were diminishing rapidly. The central flyways of migratory birds had shifted and many species of ducks and geese were gone.

Through careful conservation measures, some wildlife that had previously been eliminated from Kansas has been been brought back. Among the reinstated animals are river otters, prairie chickens, Rio Grande turkeys, antelopes, and quail. The buffalo has also been brought back, but only in very small numbers compared to the herds that once roamed the Kansas prairies.

The black-footed ferret is one of the state's most unusual endangered species. It once ranged over two-thirds of Kansas and lived in the same short-grass prairies that are home to the black-tailed prairie dog. Black-footed ferrets have not been seen in Kansas since 1957. Their disappearance is probably related to the extermination measures taken against prairie dogs.

Birds, Birds

The beautiful ring-necked pheasant was introduced into Kansas from Asia in 1905. Along with such birds as the wild turkey and the prairie chicken, which have been reintroduced into the state, pheasants are again part of Kansas's popular game-bird population.

A bird collection at Southwestern College

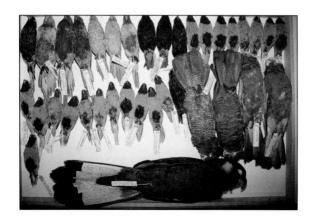

Kansas is also home to more than 400 other species of birds, including the blue jay, cardinal, robin, sparrow, owl, woodpecker, and western meadowlark—the state bird of Kansas. The bald eagle has been a resident of Kansas for hundreds of years. These majestic birds winter along the Kansas River near

Lecompton. Red-tailed hawks are the most common birds of prey in the state. Extensive bird collections are housed at the University of Kansas Museum of Natural History, at Southwestern College, and at Fort Hays State University.

The Growing Demand for Water

The Ogallala Aquifer, which underlies most of the western third of Kansas, is a huge area of water-holding rock composed mostly of sand, gravel, and silt. This important source of water underlies not only Kansas, but seven other states as well. Its average thickness is 100 feet (30 m). Millions of years of rainwater have been trapped in the aquifer.

Concerns about the aquifer are growing. Irrigating western Kansas from the aquifer is not the only reason the underground water level is dropping. There is also a greater demand for water by a growing urban population. Irrigation-conservation methods have slowed the drop in the water level in recent years, but urban areas continue to grow, and so does their need for water. Water is being removed from the aquifer much faster than it can be replenished by rain.

Kansas Climate, Kansas Weather

Kansas has three different types of climate. The eastern third of Kansas has more rainfall, higher humidity, and less sunshine than other parts of the state. The central third of the state has a higher elevation, less rainfall, more wind, and less humidity. The western third of Kansas—the High Plains—is the highest, driest, and sunniest area.

Three Years of Bad Luck

The town of Codell was hit by deadly tornadoes three years in a row—1916, 1917, and 1918. Each year the twisters hit on the same day—May 20. ▪

"We're Kansans. We live with squalls that come out of nowhere, broiling skies, hammering rain, tornadoes and tumbleweeds." A reporter penned those words following the disastrous storm of April 26, 1991, known as the Andover tornado. There were actually a series of tornadoes in Kansas that day. They caused 18 deaths and injured more than 200 people. More than 1,100 homes were destroyed, and damage was estimated in excess of $250 million.

As bad as the Andover tornado was, however, it was not the deadliest tornado in Kansas history. That tornado hit Udall on May 25, 1955, killing eighty people.

Tornadoes are not a welcome sight in Kansas.

Destruction from a
tornado in El Dorado

Between 1950 and 1995, there were 2,182 tornadoes, or cyclones, reported in Kansas. An average of 39 per year actually touch down. Although Kansas is famous for its tornadoes, such as the twister in *The Wizard of Oz,* the states of Texas and Oklahoma have more tornadoes each year than Kansas does.

Floods have also caused disasters for Kansas. The Smoky Hill Flood of 1903 poured over the town of Salina, killing 415 people. In July 1961, about 850,000 acres (343,990 ha) of farmland were submerged when the Mississippi River above St. Louis reached flood stage and stretched northward into Kansas. The death toll in that flood was twenty, with an estimated $100 million in damages.

The blizzard of 1886 that devastated the cattle industry, the dust storms of the 1930s, and the hailstorm of 1991 that blanketed Lawrence with golfball-sized hailstones have all contributed to Kansas's reputation as a state shaped by the weather.

"We learned early on that the weather demands respect," concluded the reporter covering the Andover tornado. "In Kansas, we know we are not in charge."

CHAPTER SIX

The Land of Ahs

The image most non-Kansans have of Kansas has largely been the result of a popular Hollywood movie. *The Wizard of Oz*, which first appeared in theaters in 1939, was based upon a series of fantasy books written by L. Frank Baum. He visited Kansas in the 1880s as a traveling actor.

In the story, a Kansas farm girl named Dorothy Gale and her dog, Toto, are carried away by a tornado from Kansas to the Land of Oz. The movie paints a rather bleak picture of the state, and this image became even more widespread when the film began appearing on television in 1956.

Kansas is more accurately described as "the land of ahs!" Travelers will find 133,000 miles (214,000 km) of "yellow brick roads" in Kansas, roads that can take travelers to many fascinating places.

Judy Garland played Dorothy in *The Wizard of Oz*.

Kansas's Own Kansas City

Kansas's Kansas City is just across the Missouri River from Missouri's larger Kansas City. The river can be crossed in a stern-wheeled steamboat. And such a trip is just the first adventure in a state full of adventures and fascinating sites.

Near Kansas City is Overland Park, which features the National Collegiate Athletic Association Hall of Champions. On the way is the Great Mall of the Great Plains, one of only seven superregional malls of its kind in the United States.

Opposite: Autumn at Mt. St. Scholastica in Atchison

Old Barracks at Fort Leavenworth

The hottest pop, rock, rap, hip-hop, and country stars perform under the Kansas skies at the Sandstone Amphitheater in Bonner Springs. The National Agricultural Center and Hall of Fame there features a must-see collection of old and new farm machinery.

The town of Leavenworth on the Missouri River northwest of Kansas City was the state's first incorporated town, founded in 1827. Nearby is Fort Leavenworth, the home of the oldest continuously occupied military installation west of the Mississippi River.

Heritage Hills

Straight west of Kansas City is the state capital, Topeka. Like nearby Lawrence, the city was founded by Dr. Charles Robinson and his antislavery followers. *Topeka* is an Indian word meaning something like "a good place to plant potatoes." The capitol in Topeka was built of native limestone and dates back to 1866. Wall paintings in the capitol show scenes from Kansas history, including a dramatic mural of John Brown.

The nearby Kansas Museum of History has an incredible collection of artwork and artifacts from prehistoric to present times. It also houses the Kansas Center for Historical Research. Maps, photos, and other rare materials, including the state archives, are housed here, too.

Topeka is as modern as it is historic. The 752-acre (304-ha) auto-racing facility at Heartland Park attracts visitors from around the world, and many tourists enjoy seeing the Combat Air Museum and Topeka Zoological Park.

On the campus of the University of Kansas at Lawrence are the nationally acclaimed Dyche Museum of Natural History and the Spencer Museum of Art. Baker University in Baldwin City was the first four-year college in Kansas. It began in the Old Castle, a three-story, native-limestone building constructed in 1858, which now contains a museum. The Quayle Rare Bible Collection on the Baker University campus includes a first-edition copy of the King James Bible, as well as clay tablets dating to the days before Christ.

The Old Castle Museum at Baker University

Pony Express Country

The Pony Express Museum in Marysville is housed in the only home station along the Pony Express route that is still at its original site. Marysville was the first stop after a galloping rider left St. Joseph, Missouri—the mail route's starting point.

Nearby Hiawatha is known for its lovely streets lined with hard maple trees. It is also the home of the Halloween Frolic held annually since 1914. And, yes, the town was named for the hero in Henry Wadsworth Longfellow's poem "Hiawatha."

Still Life Memorial

When Sarah Davis, the wife of Kansas farmer John Davis, died in 1930, her husband decided to build a memorial to her in Mt. Hope Cemetery. He began with two life-size, marble statues imported from Italy. He continued to add statues depicting events in the couple's life until his death in 1947. The eleven marble and granite statues cost Davis his life's savings. Each year, thousands of visitors come to see the Davis Memorial, one of the nation's most unusual private tombs. ■

Atchison, on the west bank of the Missouri River, is the birthplace of the Atchison, Topeka and Santa Fe Railroad, as well as that of America's most famous female flier, Amelia Earhart. The International Forest of Friendship in Atchison is dedicated to those contributing to the advancement of aviation. The forest has trees from all the U.S. states and U.S. territories and thirty-five other countries, as well as a tree grown from a seed that made a round-trip flight to the moon.

Post Rock Country

There are miles and miles of stone fence posts standing in Post Rock Country. This area, near a huge stone quarry from which the fence posts came, also features many houses of worship built by Russian, Czech, and German settlers. A church built by German immigrants known as the Cathedral of the Plains has twin towers soaring 140 feet (43 m) above the surrounding plains.

The Garden of Eden in Lucas is an unusual collection of concrete statues that Civil War veteran S. P. Dinsmoor built around his cabin. Dinsmoor even built his own mausoleum near his cabin. His body lies there in a glass coffin.

Cawker City claims to have the world's largest ball of twine. The ball contains more than 5,725,000 feet (1,746,125 m) of twine and weighs more than 16,800 pounds (7,627 kg). And it is still growing!

Salina boasts attractions ranging from the Salina Art Center to the unique Central Kansas Flywheel Historical Museum. A flywheel regulates the speed and motion of the machine to which it is attached.

The Record Setter from Atchison

Amelia Earhart (1897–1937?) developed a passionate interest in flying while working as a nurse's aide in Canada in 1918. She soon earned her pilot's license and began to pursue as many aviation records as she could. In 1928, she became the first woman to fly in an airplane across the Atlantic Ocean, though she was a passenger on that flight. In 1932, she earned the real record, becoming the first woman to fly alone across the Atlantic. Three years later, she became the first person—not just the first woman—to fly the long distance from Hawaii to California.

Earhart helped found the Ninety-Nines, an international organization of women pilots. She was the first woman to receive the Distinguished Flying Cross awarded by the U.S. Congress. Earhart and a navigator, Fred Noonan, attempted to fly around the world in 1937. Their airplane vanished near Howland Island in the central Pacific Ocean.

Rock City

At Rock City near Minneapolis (Kansas's Minneapolis, not Minnesota's), you can see some of Kansas's geologic history in the form of huge sandstone boulders, some as large as 27 feet (8.2 m) in diameter, strewn across the plains. The Barbed Wire Museum in LaCrosse, the Brown Grand Theatre in Concordia, and the Czech Opera House and Museum in Wilson are examples of the state's unique contributions to art and culture. Wilson also remembers Jessie Spencer. The uniform she wore as a volunteer for the American Red Cross in World War I is on display in the museum there.

Fossil Country

Fossil remains from the days when this region was covered by seas are found in huge chalk formations at Monument Rocks National Landmark. Among the fossils are those of pterosaurs—flying reptiles that took to the skies before modern birds. Fick Fossil and History Museum in Oakley contains more than 10,000 petrified shark teeth. ■

The Kansas Pueblo

El Cuartelejo, located between Oakley and Scott City at Lake Scott State Park, is the only Indian pueblo—a "town" of multistoried cliff dwellings—known to have been built in Kansas. Considered the oldest masonry building in the state, it is the northernmost pueblo built by the Taos Indians in North America nearly two centuries before European settlers arrived. After the Taos Indians moved out, the pueblo was occupied by the Picurie Indians until about 1720. The site was ignored until it was excavated in 1898. El Cuartelejo Pueblo was named a national historic landmark in 1964. A monument, the excavation site, and a museum are open to visitors. ■

The High Plains

Millions of years ago, when ancient seas rose and fell over the High Plains, valuable minerals were left buried deep in the northwest region of Kansas. The Kansas Chalk Pyramids rise south of the city of Oakley.

Kirwin National Wildlife Refuge is located near Prairie Dog State Park, which features an old adobe house and an old school. The Fort Wallace Museum shows how General George Armstrong Custer's career was affected by being stationed at this small U.S. Army fort—before he made his "last stand" at the Battle of Little Bighorn. Arikaree Breaks of Cheyenne County consists of arid canyons, spectacular pieces of natural art, surrounding the Arikaree River.

The Prairie Museum of Art and History in Colby is often called the Little Smithsonian of the West. The museum features the Kuska Collection of dolls, glass, porcelains, textiles, and furniture.

Wild West Country

When Dodge City was an important frontier town on the Santa Fe Trail, it had more than its fair share of bad guys and sheriffs. Dodge City as it was in the Wild West can be experienced at Boot Hill Museum. Kansas's largest aviation museum is located at Liberal. The Mid-America Air Museum has more than eighty vintage aircraft on display.

Garden City's Lee Richardson Zoo is one of the state's largest zoos, with more than 400 animals. Near the zoo, the largest outdoor swimming pool in the world covers half a city block and holds 2.8 million gallons (10.6 million l) of water!

The largest area of public land in Kansas is the 108,175-acre (43,270-ha) Cimarron National Grasslands near Elkhart. Part of the Dust Bowl of the 1930s, the area has been reclaimed as a complete ecosystem of native wildlife and plants.

Fort Larned National Historic Site is regarded as one of the best-preserved places along the old Santa Fe Trail. Originally built to protect travelers on the trail, it became the center of the army's attempt to conquer the Plains Indians.

Fort Larned National Historic Site

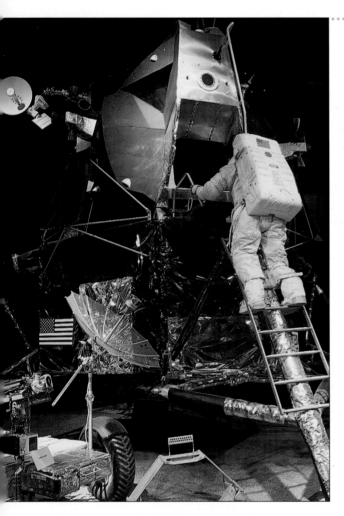

A lunar module at the Kansas Cosmosphere and Space Center

Heartland Country

Soviet cosmonaut Svetlana Savitskaya's name isn't readily recognized in Kansas, or anywhere else in the United States. In 1984, she became the first woman to walk in space. Some of the clothing she wore is one of the prized exhibits at the Kansas Cosmosphere and Space Center in Hutchinson. The Cosmosphere has the largest display of Russian space memorabilia in the world outside of Moscow. Hutchinson is also the home of the Kansas State Fair.

Just south of Hutchinson is the Amish community of Yoder. The influence of Mennonite settlers is documented in museums in Hillsboro, North Newton, and Goessel.

The town of Lindsborg is known as Little Sweden U.S.A. The Birger Sandzen Memorial Gallery on the campus of Bethany College features many of the works of this famous Swedish-American painter who taught at Bethany.

Quivira National Wildlife Refuge near Stafford is a favorite of bird-watchers. The Coronado-Quivira Museum in Lyons displays artifacts from Coronado's 1541 trip to Kansas and from the period of Spanish exploration.

The Peace Treaty Pageant is held every three years in Medicine Lodge. More than 1,500 people help stage the pageant, which re-enacts the Indian way of life in Kansas.

Pancakes

Every February, the town of Liberal, in far western Kansas, holds the International Pancake Derby. Local housewives compete with women from Liberal's sister city—Olney, England. They run a 1/4-mile (400-m) race while carrying pancakes in heavy skillets and flipping them at the beginning and end of the race. Competitors must be female, between the ages of twenty-five and fifty-two, and must race in skirts or dresses, aprons, and headscarves. The tradition began in Olney. In 1950, a charitable organization in Liberal proposed that Olney and Liberal hold an international pancake competition. Since then, the two cities have been keeping track of race scores and sending representatives to observe each other's races.

Ingredients:

1 1/4 cup flour

1 teaspoon of salt

4 tablespoons of sugar

2 eggs

1 1/4 cups of milk

Directions:

Combine all the ingredients, in a blender and blend until mixed thoroughly. The batter should be smooth. Preheat a heavy skillet. You can test to make sure the skillet is hot enough by splashing a few drops of water on it. If the water slides around on the pan before evaporating, then the skillet is ready.

Carefully pour the batter onto the skillet to make circles, about 5 inches (13 cm) in diameter. Fit as many pancakes onto the pan as possible. When the batter bubbles, check the undersides by lifting up the side of a pancake with a spatula. When the undersides are golden brown, turn the pancakes. The other sides will take only half as long to cook.

Top with butter and syrup, if desired.

To get an idea of how difficult the Liberal-Olney race is, make a skillet-sized pancake. When it is ready to flip, hold the skillet well away from the burner, and try flipping the pancake without using a spatula.

Serves 4.

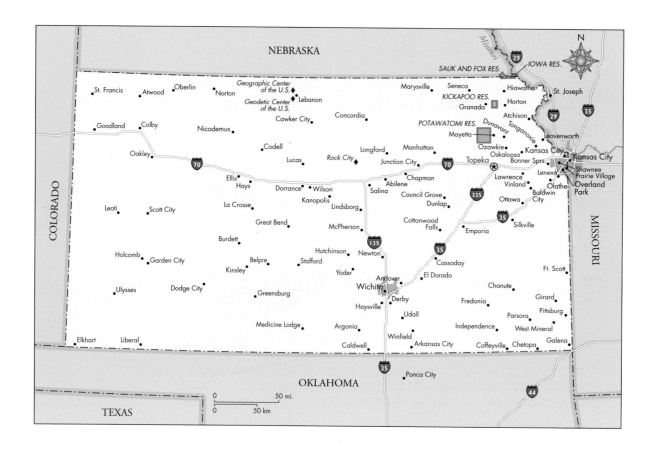

Wichita Area

From Old Cowtown Museum to the Wichita Center for the Arts, there are treasures galore in Wichita. Rated as Wichita favorites in a recent visitors' survey were the Children's Museum of Wichita, the Wichita Art Museum, and the Edwin A. Ulrich Museum of Art, which houses the largest collection of contemporary art west of the Mississippi River. Another favorite is the Mid-America All-Indian Center and Museum featuring permanent collections of the people of the plains.

Wichita is considered the Air Capital of the World because of its massive production of aircraft, both large and small. Flying can be fun in Wichita without ever leaving the ground at the Omnisphere and Science Center and the Kansas Aviation Museum.

Flint Hills

The Flint Hills area was the place where Plains Indians got the stone called flint, or chert, that they used to make arrowheads and tools. Some of the area is original prairieland that has never been plowed. The Konza Prairie near Manhattan is the largest protected

The Konza Prairie

The Kansas Sage

William Allen White (1868–1944) was born in Emporia and grew up in El Dorado. When his father died, fourteen-year-old White went to work learning the newspaper business. He and his wife, Sally Lindsay White, purchased the *Emporia Daily and Weekly Gazette* in 1895.

White became a best-selling novelist and was awarded a Pulitzer Prize for his editorial "To an Anxious Friend," defending freedom of speech. An earlier editorial, "What's the Matter with Kansas?" brought him national fame and helped get William McKinley elected president. White wrote biographies of famous Americans, but his tribute following the sudden death of his daughter, Mary, in 1921 remains his best-known piece of writing. ■

Kansas "Capitals"

- Haysville, Peach Capital
- Parsons, Purple Martin Capital
- Marysville, Black Squirrel Capital
- Cassody, Prairie Chicken Capital
- Norton, Pheasant Capital
- Chetopa, Catfish Capital
- Leoti, Pinto Bean Capital
- Yates Center, Hay Capital

tallgrass prairie in the United States. It is a photographer's paradise of beautiful wildflowers and other natural works of art.

Although many of the legends of the Wild West began in Abilene, today's Abilene is dedicated to President Dwight D. Eisenhower. The complex of his home, library, and burial site is the state's most popular tourist attraction. Nearby is the Warren Hall Coutts III Memorial Museum of Art, which features more than 1,000 works of art and antique furniture pieces.

Emporia, known as "the front porch to the Flint Hills," is the home of the National Teachers Hall of Fame. The former home of Pulitzer Prize–winning journalist William Allen White is another favorite stop in Emporia.

Little Ozarks

In ancient times, this area was a bog. It now contains rich veins of coal. For years the coal was strip-mined by Big Brutus, an

11-million-pound (5-million-kg) mechanical shovel. In one swoop, it could gather enough rock and dirt to fill three railroad cars. Big Brutus is now part of a museum of mining near West Mineral.

You can take a safari in Kansas with a visit to the Martin and Osa Johnson Safari Museum in Chanute. This museum celebrates the exploits of two pioneering wildlife photographers who shot remarkable documentary films between 1917 and 1936 from the South Seas to Africa.

Children of all ages enjoy visiting the Emmett Kelly Museum in Sedan, which honors America's most beloved clown. The sad-faced clown who made people unsure whether to laugh or cry was born in Sedan. But Willie, his clown character, was born in Kansas City, where Emmett Kelly worked in advertising before joining the circus.

With so many interesting places to see and enjoy, it's easy to see why Dorothy and Toto wanted to return to Kansas.

Putting a Spell on Kansas

Konza is one of the more than one hundred ways *Kansas* has been spelled. Some of the other spellings that appeared on maps between 1650 and 1854 were *Okanes*, *Excausaquex*, *Canses*, and *Karsea*. ■

CHAPTER SEVEN

Governing Kansas

The Kansas House of Representatives in session, 1923

No other document is as important to modern Kansas as its constitution. While other states have had many constitutions, Kansas has had only one since it became a state.

The Kansas constitution was patterned after the constitution of Ohio. It is called the Wyandotte Constitution because Wyandotte was the place where delegates convened on July 5, 1859, to compose the document that was approved by Congress. It is the constitution under which Kansas was admitted to the United States.

The Kansas constitution has been amended more than eighty times. Any amendment to the constitution must be approved by two-thirds of both houses of the state legislature, plus a majority of statewide voters. In spite of the amendments made to the Kansas constitution since 1859, the government of Kansas has not changed significantly since Kansas became a state.

The Executive Branch

Kansas, like the federal government, has three separate branches of government—executive, legislative, and judicial. Each branch acts as a balance for the other branches so that no one branch can become too powerful.

The governor is the chief officer of the executive branch. The

Opposite: The Kansas state capitol

Kansas's Governors

Name	Party	Term	Name	Party	Term
Charles Robinson	Rep.	1861–1863	Jonathan M. Davis	Dem.	1923–1925
Thomas Carney	Rep.	1863–1865	Ben S. Paulen	Rep.	1925–1929
Samuel J. Crawford	Rep.	1865–1868	Clyde M. Reed	Rep.	1929–1931
Nehemiah Green	Rep.	1868–1869	Harry H. Woodring	Dem.	1931–1933
James M. Harvey	Rep.	1869–1873	Alfred M. Landon	Rep.	1933–1937
Thomas A. Osborn	Rep.	1873–1877	Walter A. Huxman	Dem.	1937–1939
George T. Anthony	Rep.	1877–1879	Payne Ratner	Rep.	1939–1943
John Pierce St. John	Rep.	1879–1883	Andrew F. Schoeppel	Rep.	1943–1947
George W. Glick	Dem.	1883–1885	Frank Carlson	Rep.	1947–1950
John Alexander Martin	Rep.	1885–1889	Frank L. Hagaman	Rep.	1950–1951
Lyman Underwood Humphrey	Rep.	1889–1893	Edward F. Arn	Rep.	1951–1955
			Fred Hall	Rep.	1955–1957
Lorenzo D. Lewelling	Pop.	1893–1895	John McCuish	Rep.	1957
Edmund Needham Morrill	Rep.	1895–1897	George Docking	Dem.	1957–1961
John W. Leedy	Pop.	1897–1899	John Anderson Jr.	Rep.	1961–1965
William Eugene Stanley	Rep.	1899–1903	William H. Avery	Rep.	1965–1967
Willis Joshua Bailey	Rep.	1903–1905	Robert Docking	Dem.	1967–1975
Edward Wallis Hoch	Rep.	1905–1909	Robert F. Bennett	Rep.	1975–1979
Walter Roscoe Stubbs	Rep.	1909–1913	John W. Carlin	Dem.	1979–1987
George Hartshorn Hodges	Dem.	1913–1915	Mike Hayden	Rep.	1987–1991
Arthur Capper	Rep.	1915–1919	Joan Finney	Dem.	1991–1995
Henry J. Allen	Rep.	1919–1923	Bill Graves	Rep.	1995–

laws of the state are administered, and the policies and programs required in modern government are carried out, through the executive departments, agencies, boards, and commissions.

Other elected officers serve with the governor in the executive branch. These include the lieutenant governor, secretary of state, state treasurer, attorney general, and commissioner of insurance. All are elected to four-year terms. The governor and lieutenant governor may serve an unlimited number of terms, but no more than two consecutive terms.

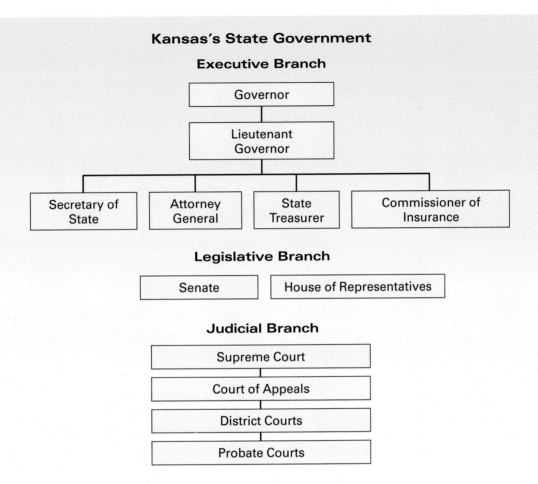

Kansas's State Government

Executive Branch

Governor

Lieutenant Governor

| Secretary of State | Attorney General | State Treasurer | Commissioner of Insurance |

Legislative Branch

Senate   House of Representatives

Judicial Branch

Supreme Court

Court of Appeals

District Courts

Probate Courts

The Legislative Branch

The legislative branch makes the laws of the state. It consists of a 40-member senate, and a 125-member house of representatives. The lieutenant governor is president of the senate. The house elects its own presiding officer. Kansas state senators are elected to four-year terms. Kansas state representatives are elected to two-year terms.

Kansas is represented in the U.S. Congress by two senators and four representatives. The state has six electoral votes.

Political Firsts for Kansas Women

1887 Susanna Madora Salter elected mayor of Argonia, the first woman to be elected mayor of a town in the United States.

1918 Minnie Grinstead, first woman elected to the Kansas legislature.

1932 Kathryn O'Loughlin, first Kansas woman elected to the U.S. House of Representatives.

1949 Georgia Neese Clark Gray, first woman appointed U.S. treasurer.

1978 Nancy Landon Kassebaum (above), first woman elected to represent Kansas in the U.S. Senate.

The Judicial Branch

The judicial branch is topped by the supreme court, with a chief justice and six other justices. All are initially appointed to the court by the governor. The governor decides who to appoint based upon a list submitted by the Supreme Court Nominating Commission. Voters then decide whether to retain the new judge. The chief justice is the justice who has served on the court longest.

Kansas has a court of appeals made up of ten members elected to four-year terms. The state also has thirty-one district courts. Judges on these courts are elected to four-year terms. Two Kansans have served on the U.S. Supreme Court as justices: David Brewer, who served from 1890 to 1910, and Charles Whittaker, who served from 1957 to 1962.

Kansas Issues

Government spending in Kansas still follows a cash-basis law passed in 1933 during Governor Alfred M. Landon's administration. Landon was defeated in his later bid for the presidency, but Kansans continue to use his "pay as you grow" program.

In his 1998 State of the State address to the legislature, Governor Bill Graves said, "We must not deviate from these conservative policies. We cannot spend money we do not have, nor spend money we hope will be there. There is no Kansas credit card."

Recent political issues in Kansas have centered on social services, taxes, prison reforms, highway improvement, environmental and natural resources, juvenile crime, legalized gambling and, once again, liquor sales. In 1986, constitutional amendments allowed certain types of betting, a state lottery, and liquor by the drink. However, each of Kansas's 105 counties is allowed to decide for itself whether to allow liquor by the drink.

Thirty-fourth President from the Thirty-fourth State

"I Like Ike" slogans swept the nation like a Kansas prairie fire in 1952. Dwight David Eisenhower (1890–1969) was a Kansas-raised boy who served during World War II and led Allied troops to victory in the D-day invasion of Europe. His popularity as a leader was enormous.

Eisenhower was born in Denison, Texas. When he was one year old, his parents moved the family to Abilene, Kansas. He

Governor Bill Graves

The Kansas Vice President

Charles Curtis (1860–1936), a native of North Topeka (now Topeka) was the thirty-first vice president of the United States. He is the only person of Indian descent ever to hold this office.

From 1893 to 1907, Curtis served in the U.S. House of Representatives. He then served in the U.S. Senate. Herbert Hoover, the Republican presidential candidate in 1928, chose Curtis as his running mate and they won overwhelmingly. Curtis was the first Kansan to hold a major national office. ■

County Names

Of the 105 counties in Kansas, 47 are named for Civil War veterans. There are 17 counties with Indian names. Barton County is the only Kansas county named for a woman. It honors Clara Barton, a famous nurse of the U.S. Civil War (1861–1865). ■

A familiar sight in Kansas during the 1952 presidential elections

Kansas's counties

excelled in sports in high school and received an appointment to West Point, the U.S. military academy. While stationed in the army in Texas, he met Mamie Doud and they were married in 1916.

In his early military career, Eisenhower proved to be a wise, strong leader. After World War II ended, he became the president of Columbia University, then assumed command over the North Atlantic Treaty Organization (NATO) forces. In 1952, he ran for president as a Republican and won a solid victory.

During his eight years as president, Eisenhower concentrated on maintaining world peace in the midst of growing tension between Western nations and the Soviet Union. He advocated negotiating from a position of military strength.

"While history remembers him as a soldier who became the nation's commander in chief, Kansans remember Dwight Eisenhower as the boy from Kansas who made us proud to be Kansans, too," said former Kansas senator Robert Dole during his own campaign for the presidency in 1996. Although Dole was not successful in his bid, he too has made Kansans proud through his service in both the U.S. Senate and the House of Representatives.

Kansas's State Flag, Seal, and Motto

The first official Kansas state flag was adopted in 1927. It consists of a sunflower atop the state seal on a blue background. Directly beneath the sunflower is a blue and gold bar signifying Kansas as part of the Louisiana Purchase. The word "Kansas" was added to the flag in 1961.

For two years before the state flag was approved, Kansas was represented by an official state banner. The silk banner was 21 inches wide by 28 inches high (53 by 71 cm). It had a royal blue field adorned with the word "Kansas" at the top, and a centered sunflower surrounding the state seal.

The seal shows a landscape with a rising sun, representing the East. A river and steamboat represent commerce. In the foreground, a settler's cabin and a man plowing a field represent agriculture. A wagon train heads west, and buffalo are seen fleeing from two Native Americans. Around the top of the seal is a cluster of thirty-four stars. The state motto—*Ad Astra per Aspera* ("To the Stars through Difficulties")—appears above the stars. ■

Kansas's State Symbols

State Flower: Wild sunflower (left) In spite of objections that it is actually a weed and not a flower, the 1903 session of the legislature made it the official state flower of Kansas.

State tree: Eastern cottonwood It is often called the "pioneer of Kansas" because of its abundance on the plains and its willingness to grow where there is little water. The state's largest cottonwood tree is located on federal land southwest of Ozawkie. It measures more than 28 feet (8.5 m) around the trunk and stands over 111 feet (34 m) tall. It was adopted in 1937.

State insect: Honeybee Like farmers everywhere, Kansas farmers know the importance of the honeybee, so it became the state insect in 1976.

State amphibian: Barred tiger salamander Adopted in 1973, this striped amphibian lives in moist, dark places, usually along rivers.

State animal: American buffalo The plains of western Kansas were once filled with huge herds of bison. The American buffalo was adopted in 1955.

State reptile: Ornate box turtle (below left) In 1986, students in Caldwell led the effort to have it adopted as the state reptile. Also called the western box turtle, it has a flatter top shell than most box turtles.

State bird: Western meadowlark The bird was selected in 1937 based upon votes cast by the schoolchildren of Kansas in 1925. The intricate whistle of the western meadowlark sounds across the plains.

State soil: Harney silt loam Kansas is one of only seven states to have chosen a state soil. Harney silt loam, adopted in 1990, covers almost 4 million acres (1.6 million ha) in twenty-six west-central Kansas counties. The name *Harney* is adapted from the ancient Wichita Indian word *harahey*, meaning "Pawnee people."

State march: "The Kansas March" Composed by Duff E. Middleton, the march is different from the familiar state song. It was adopted in 1935.

Kansas's State Song
"Home on the Range" (originally "My Western Home")

Lyrics by Brewster Higley; music by Daniel Kelley.
Brewster Higley was a frontier doctor and homesteader in Smith County. The poem was published in the Smith County newspaper, *The Pioneer,* in December 1873. Daniel Kelley was a member of a popular musical group in nearby Gaylord. By 1930, the song had appeared in at least ten sheet-music editions.

Oh, give me a home where the buffalo roam,
Where the deer and the antelope play,
Where seldom is heard a discouraging word
And the skies are not cloudy all day.

Chorus:
Home, home on the range
Where the deer and the antelope play,
Where seldom is heard a discouraging word
And the skies are not cloudy all day.
Where the air is so pure, the zephyrs so free,
The breezes so balmy and light
That I would not exchange my home on the range
For all of the cities so bright.

The red man was pressed from this part of the West,
He's likely no more to return
To the banks of Red River where seldom if ever
Their flickering campfires burn.

(Chorus)

How often at night when the heavens are bright
With the light from the glittering stars,
Have I stood here amazed and asked as I gazed
If their glory exceeds that of ours.

(Chorus)

Oh, I love these wild flowers in this dear land of ours,
The curlew I love to hear scream,

And I love the white rocks and the antelope flocks
That graze on the mountain-tops green.

(Chorus)

Oh, give me a land where the bright diamond sand
Flows leisurely down the stream,
Where the graceful white swan goes gliding along
Like a maid in a heavenly dream.

(Chorus)

Then I would not exchange my home on the range,
Where the deer and the antelope play;
Where seldom is heard a discouraging word
And the skies are not cloudy all day.

CHAPTER EIGHT

Working in Kansas

JOHN DEERE 95

Kansas has one of the fastest-growing economies in the United States today. One-fourth of all Kansas graduates are now preparing to enter the workforce, and they probably won't have any trouble finding a job. Jobs in manufacturing, services and retail trade, and agribusiness will be filled by people with skills, education, and a strong work ethic—the willingness to work hard and the belief that work is important. A strong work ethic is what enabled the pioneers to settle Kansas.

Sprint Communications is headquartered in Kansas.

The state's central location makes it a major hub in the nation's transportation system. Highway 54, which crosses the state from Fort Scott through Wichita down to Liberal, is designated the official Yellow Brick Road in Kansas. It is just a part of the state's transportation system of highways, railroads, and airports that help to move the Kansas economy.

Kansas invests more than $200 million each year to prepare for future business growth. Sprint Communications, which began in Abilene as Brown Telephone Company, is one of the nation's leading communications companies. Sprint is part of the reason Kansas has become one of the top ten states in the percentage of its workforce employed in high-tech industries.

Opposite: Harvesting crops in the Sunflower State

Top Nine Kansas Companies in 1997
(Ranked by number of employees)

1. Sprint/United Telephone; Telecommunications
2. The Boeing Company; Aircraft Manufacturing
3. Raytheon Aircraft Company; Aircraft Manufacturing
4. IBP, Inc.; Meatpacking
5. Burlington Northern Santa Fe Corporation; Railroad
6. Cessna Aircraft Company; Aircraft Manufacturing
7. General Motors; Automobile Manufacturing
8. Western Resources; Electric & Gas Utility
9. Southwestern Bell; Telecommunications

(Source: Kansas Department of Commerce and Housing)

Lloyd Stearman

Impact of the Aviation Industry

In the early days of aviation, not many people were willing to take a chance on the new-fangled flying machines, but Kansas had a lot of farsighted residents. They included such early aviation businesspeople as A. K. Longren, E. M. Laird, Clyde Cessna, Walter Beech, Lloyd Stearman, and J. M. Mollendick. Today, aviation-related industries employ 22 percent of all the manufacturing workers in Kansas.

The Big Four in the Air

There are four major aircraft companies in Kansas. In 1996, they spent a combined total of more than $2.4 billion in the state.

The Boeing Company became the largest aerospace company in the world in 1997. Boeing is the largest manufacturer of commercial jetliners and military aircraft and the nation's largest contractor for the National Aeronautics and Space Administration (NASA). Although its headquarters are in the Seattle, Washington, area, Boeing has built aircraft in Kansas for decades.

Cessna Aircraft opened its newest manufacturing facility at Independence to increase its production of piston-engine aircraft. It is the largest producer of general aviation aircraft in the United States. (General aviation aircraft are all airplanes other than commercial airliners and military airplanes.)

Kansas Aviation Firsts

- The first Kansas airplane manufacturer was Henry Call of Girard.
- William Purvis patented the first helicopter in Goodland in 1910.
- A. K. Longren built and flew the first airplane in Kansas in 1911.
- Claude Ryan, born in Parsons, designed and built the *Spirit of St. Louis,* the airplane flown by Charles Lindbergh in his famous 1927 solo flight across the Atlantic Ocean.

Building airplanes at Boeing in Wichita

The Man Who Loved Airplanes

Clyde Vernon Cessna (1879–1954) was a wheat farmer who saw his first aerial exhibition in Kansas in 1911. It sparked his lifelong dedication to aviation. He designed and built his own airplane and taught himself to fly.

In 1925, he and Walter Beech started the Travel Air Manufacturing Company in Wichita. With Cessna as its president, the company became one of the leading U.S. aircraft manufacturers. He then formed the Cessna Aircraft Company. Cessna's airplanes set standards for safety, performance, and economy that are still followed by airplane manufacturers today. ■

Kansans in Space

■ Ron Evans (above) of St. Francis and Topeka was commander of the pilot ship during the flight of *Apollo 17* to the moon.

■ Steve Hawley of Ottawa and Salina carried Kansas flags on the maiden flight of the space shuttle *Discovery*.
■ Joe Engle of Chapman flew on the maiden voyage of the space shuttle *Columbia.*
■ Clyde Tombaugh of Burdett was an early "space traveler." Working at an observatory in Arizona, he discovered the planet Pluto in 1930.

Learjet Inc., is a leading maker of corporate jets. The company was started by William Lear, who designed the first car radios and many of the navigational instruments used in aircraft. Lear also designed the eight-track tape player that was popular in the 1960s.

Raytheon Aircraft Company designs and manufactures many aviation-related electronic and computer systems. The company produces Beech Aircraft, started by Walter Beech and his wife, Olive. Raytheon supplies special-mission aircraft to the U.S. government and its allies.

More Manufacturing Marvels

Not everything manufactured in Kansas has wings or flies. Reuter pipe organs built in Lawrence are highly prized by musicians. Giant dump-truck tires, each 12 feet (3.7 m) in diameter and weighing 12,500 pounds (5,670 kg), are made by the Goodyear Company in Topeka. The Coleman Company, headquartered in Wichita, makes and sells everything one needs for camping.

Koch Industries petrochemicals and General Motors automobiles are just a few of the industries supplying the world with Kansas-made products. Shoppers come to Kansas to buy specialty items such as Kansas-made quilts, hand puppets, Swedish Dala horses, cowboy boots, and other unique items.

Inside the Coleman Company

Awesome Agribusiness

Kansans are a major part of the 21 million people working in agriculture in the United States. Every year, each farmer in Kansas provides food and fiber for 129 people—97 in the United States and 32 abroad.

The first European settlers who planted corn in Kansas used axes to chop holes in the ground, and then they dropped in three kernels of corn. They chopped the holes about 3 feet (1 m) apart and then stepped on the hole to cover the corn with dirt. By 1919, there were 1.3 million farm animals pulling plows and planters and reapers across Kansas. Within seventeen years, half of those animals had been replaced by farm tractors and combines.

Animals continued to be essential to Kansas farm production until after World War II. Today, a new piece of farm machinery can cost as much as 200 farm horses cost in 1914. By 1997, high-tech

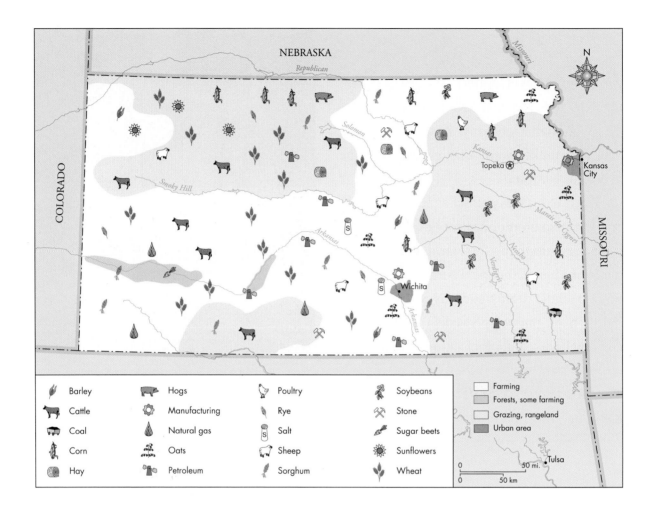

								Farming
Barley		Hogs		Poultry		Soybeans		Forests, some farming
Cattle		Manufacturing		Rye		Stone		Grazing, rangeland
Coal		Natural gas		Salt		Sugar beets		Urban area
Corn		Oats		Sheep		Sunflowers		
Hay		Petroleum		Sorghum		Wheat		

Kansas's natural resources

farming helped Kansas farmers set new records in wheat, corn, and soybean production. However, the prices they received for these crops averaged 30 percent less then prices in 1996.

Kansas regained its status as the number-one wheat-producing state in the nation in 1997 after losing to North Dakota the previous two years. It retained its title as the number-one producer of sorghum grain for the eighth straight year. Soybean and corn crops set new production records.

There were just over 6.5 million head of cattle in Kansas on January 1, 1998. That's about 2.7 cows for each person living in Kansas. Texas has more cattle, but by comparison there are only 1.1 cows per person in Texas.

Beef cattle in a Kansas pasture

The Census of Agriculture

The Census of Agriculture is conducted nationwide every five years. It provides a snapshot of agriculture in the United States and is used for assessing trends and determining the current needs of farmers and ranchers. The 1997 census revealed the following Kansas crop-production statistics:

Crop	Acres Harvested (in millions)	Bushels Harvested (in millions)	Total Value
Wheat	11.0	506	$1.619 billion
Corn	2.7	386	1.023 billion
Grain sorghum	3.5	273	587 million
Soybeans	2.4	89	573 million

In 1997, Kansas produced enough wheat to make more than 30 billion loaves of bread. That would make about six loaves for each person on Earth. ■

What Kansas Grows, Manufactures, and Mines

Agriculture	Manufacturing	Mining
Beef cattle	Transportation equipment	Petroleum
Wheat	Food products	Natural gas
Corn	Printed materials	
Grain sorghum	Machinery	
Hay	Rubber and plastics products	
Hogs		
Soybeans		

More than two-thirds of Kansas's agricultural products go to feed the world. Exports were worth $2.7 billion in 1997. Kansas ranked first among the states in the value of its wheat exports, third in the value of meat, and third in the value of sunflower seeds and oil.

Manufacturing surpassed agriculture as the largest source of income in Kansas in 1953, but agriculture is still big business in Kansas. A huge beef-processing complex near Garden City was opened by Iowa Beef Packers (IBP), Inc., in 1980. IBP, Inc., is the largest U.S. exporter of red meat and related products. IBP's allied product line produces more than 250 by products from cattle parts not used for food. Cattle hides for making leather goods are IBP's best-known allied product.

Other Products from the Ground

Mineral production in Kansas offers fewer job opportunities today than it did in the past. However, these jobs in the overall economy of Kansas continue to be important in the state's future. For exam-

The Silk Makers

In the late 1860s, Frenchman Ernest Valeton de Boissiere helped bring French immigrants to Kansas to start a silk factory. The factory's looms produced as much as 300 yards (275 m) of finished material a day in 1869. His factory proved to be unprofitable, and the town of Silkville turned to dairying to survive. Silk was produced in forty Kansas counties from 1889 to 1900. ▪

Phillipsburg Oil Refinery

ple, stone, salt, and helium worth $495 million were produced in Kansas in 1994.

Kansas consistently ranks among the top ten oil-producing states. What the long-term effects of the ups and downs in the oil and gas industry will be on Kansas remains to be seen. One thing is certain: Job opportunities in Kansas will continue to require skill, education, and a strong work ethic. According to a member of the Kansas State Chamber of Commerce, "Regardless of what kind of work you want to do, there is a place under the Kansas sun for you."

CHAPTER NINE

Modern People of the Plains

"T he question is, by whom shall these plains be inhabited?" That question was asked in a report by an explorer after his 1835 travels in Kansas territory. It is doubtful that he, or any of the early explorers and settlers, ever imagined there would be people called Hmong from the countries of Southeast Asia living in Kansas today. The Hmong are part of the 1.3 percent of Kansas's Asian/Pacific Islander population. Most of the Hmong have come to Kansas since 1980.

Immigrant wagons in Topeka during the 1870s

Descendants of immigrants from Illinois, Iowa, and Kentucky as well as pioneers brought by the New England Emigrant Aid Society were among the first settlers to populate Kansas. They were followed by German, Russian, British, Swiss, Belgian, French, Swedish, and Norwegian immigrants. Their descendants make up most of the 90 percent of the state's approximately 2.5 million residents who are white.

African-Americans make up 5.8 percent of the population. Hispanics, who rarely lived in Kansas before 1900, account for 3.8 percent. By 1990, one-fourth of Kansas's foreign-born population came from Mexico.

Approximately 6 percent of Kansans speak languages other than English at home. The ten most common languages spoken,

Opposite: A hula hoop contest

The Pioneer Child

Daniel Morgan Boone, son of famed frontiersman Daniel Boone, settled in Kansas in 1827. He came to teach better farming methods to Native Americans in the Fort Leavenworth area. His son, Napoleon, is believed to be the first white child born in Kansas. ■

A festival celebrating Native American culture in Lenexa

other than English, are Spanish, German, French, Vietnamese, Chinese, Korean, Lao, Arabic, Japanese, and Italian.

Immigrants Then and Now

Between 1990 and 1993, more than 3,200 immigrants from other countries came to the United States and chose Kansas to be their home. Earlier immigrants, however, came as a result of the Indian Removal Bill of 1830. This law forced more than 80,000 Indians east of the Mississippi River to move to territories in Kansas, Oklahoma, and Nebraska. Kansas has since been the home, at various times, of Arapaho, Cherokee, Cheyenne, Comanche, Delaware, Flathead, Illinois, Kansa, Kiowa, Miami, Osage, Oto,

Pawnee, Peoria, Piankashaw, Quapay, Wea, Wichita, and Yskani people.

Less than 1 percent of the Kansas population today is Native American. Only about 22,000 Fox, Iowa, Kickapoo, Ottawa, Potawatomi, Sauk, Shawnee, Cherokee, and Wyandot Indians now live in the state.

Where Kansans Live

If the people of Kansas were spread evenly across the state, there would be only 30 people per square mile (12 people per sq km). Compare that to Florida, where there would be 222 people per square mile (86 people per sq km) to see why Kansas is still con-

Population Increases

The state's population did not reach 2 million until the 1960 census. The population increased by 121,364 people (4.9 percent) between 1980 and 1990. The Census Bureau population projection is 2,722,000 for the year 2000, and 2,922,000 for 2010. ■

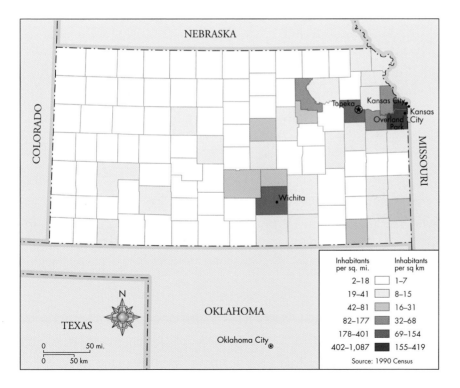

Kansas's population density

Population of Kansas's Major Cities (1990)

Wichita	304,011
Kansas City	149,767
Topeka	119,883
Overland Park	111,790
Lawrence	65,608
Olathe	63,352

Educating Kansans

The first schools in Kansas were religious missions among the Indians. A law requiring children between the ages of eight and fourteen to attend school was passed in 1874. During the next decade, Kansas became the first state to require drug education, warning students of the dangers of alcohol and narcotics. ■

Preparing for Tribal Life

Haskell Indian Nations University in Lawrence opened in 1884 as an elementary school for Indian children. It eventually became a high school, and then a college. More than 900 students representing 147 tribes were enrolled in 1998. Courses in tribal management are among its specialized studies. ■

sidered a rural state even though only 31 percent of the people live in rural areas.

Greely County in western Kansas is the least populated county. It had 1,754 people in 1996, while Sedgwick County, the most populated, had 422,436. Only four cities in Kansas have a population of more than 100,000: Wichita, Topeka, Kansas City, and Overland Park. There are thirty-four cities of 10,000 or more.

In 1930, Johnson County had 452 residents. By 1970, the population had reached 5,242. In the twenty years between 1970 and 1990, the population grew to an amazing 33,833, making it the fastest-growing county in the state of Kansas. This growth is due to the increasing number of new jobs in manufacturing and technology in the Kansas City area.

Segregation in schools, which sent black children and white children to different facilities, was practiced in Kansas. Kansas did not fully integrate its schools until several years after the decision by the U.S. Supreme Court in the 1954 *Brown* v. *Topeka Board of Education* case. This 1954 ruling dissolved the right of school districts to have separate schools based upon race.

There were 468,744 students in Kansas schools in 1997. Special-education classes were available for three- and four-year-olds. Kansas was the third state to mandate kindergarten for all children.

Eighty-two percent of Kansas's students graduate from high school. About 20 percent of the high school graduates go on to attend a college or university.

The first institution of higher learning in Kansas was Highland College, established in 1858. Kansas now has fifty-two colleges and universities. Emporia State in Emporia, Fort Hays State in Hays, Kansas State in Manhattan and Salina, Wichita State in Wichita, Pittsburg State in Pittsburg, and the University of Kansas in Lawrence are among the largest. In 1866, the University of Kansas became the first state-run institution of higher learning in Kansas to admit women.

Private schools and colleges are found throughout Kansas. Bethel College in North Newton is the oldest Mennonite college in the United States. Friends University in Wichita, affiliated with the Quaker Church, is the largest independent college in Kansas.

An Important Pioneer

Lutie Lytle (1874–?), who graduated from Topeka High School, became the first African-American female licensed attorney in the United States in 1897. She was also the first female attorney to appear before the U.S. Supreme Court. ■

One of the many buildings at the University of Kansas in Lawrence

Other private schools include Baker University in Baldwin City, Benedictine College in Atchison, Bethany College in Lindsborg, McPherson College in McPherson, Newman College in Wichita, and Nazarene College in Olathe.

The News in Kansas

Jotham Meeker, a missionary, established the first newspaper published in Kansas. The first copy of the *Shawnee Sun* appeared on February 24, 1835. The newspaper, a monthly publication, was printed in the native language of the Shawnee people.

"The printing press led, rather than followed, the course of progress in Kansas," said Tom McNeal. He was considered the "dean" of Kansas editors in 1938. For six years, McNeal held the office of state printer. He believed editors such as William Allen White, John Ingalls, Noble L. Prentis, Marshall Murdock, and Arthur Capper (who became governor of Kansas in 1915) "left their signatures not only upon editorials, but upon Kansas."

In a 1937 survey, there had already been 4,368 newspapers published in Kansas—more than in any other state. There are currently more than 260 daily or weekly newspapers published in the state. They range from the *Abilene Reflector-Chronicle* to the *Yates Center News*. The *Wichita Eagle-Beacon* has the largest circulation. Many of these newspapers are available on the Internet.

The first commercial radio station in Kansas was KFH in Wichita, which began broadcasting in 1922. The first commercial

Remembering a Country Teacher

Lydia Mayfield of Halstead remembers her first-grade teacher very well and has written about her: "It was just before World War I. We lived on a farm in western Kansas. Miss Flo Akins, my first-grade teacher, was only fifteen years old! She was smaller than some of her eighth-grade pupils in our one-room school, and just a few months older. She had graduated from eighth grade, then attended a two-week institute in the county seat to become a teacher. She was in charge of educating twenty youngsters, ages five to fourteen.

"Despite her youth, Miss Akins ran the school with discipline. At the end of my first-grade year, the school board asked Miss Akins to stay on. She declined, deciding instead to go to high school." ■

television station was KTVH in Hutchinson in 1953. By 1990, Kansas had 175 commercial and educational radio stations as well as 20 commercial and educational TV stations.

Keeping Kansas Healthy

While the Kansas population increased nearly 25 percent between 1900 and the late 1940s, the number of physicians decreased by 30 percent. To solve this problem, Dr. Franklin D. Murphy, dean of the University of Kansas Medical School, developed a plan for helping young doctors in isolated rural communities. This led to the state legislature adopting the Kansas Rural Health Bill in 1949.

Within a few years, every Kansas county and every community with a population of more than 1,000 had at least one doctor. Again, the number of doctors and hospitals in Kansas's rural communities is declining. Addressing this problem is a priority with many Kansans.

Charles Menninger (center) with his sons William (left) and Karl

Outstanding Kansans in Medicine

- Earl Sutherland (above) was awarded the Nobel Prize in 1971 for his human hormone discoveries.
- Elmer McCollum discovered vitamins A, B, D, and E.
- Takera Higuchi invented the time-release capsule, which releases medicine into the body throughout the day.

Kansas is famous for its health-care programs for the mentally ill. Topeka is known internationally as the home of the Menninger Foundation, a nonprofit organization dedicated to the study of mental illness. Charles Menninger and his son Karl opened a group psychiatric practice in 1925 and were soon joined by Karl's brother, William. Their practice became the center for the treatment of mental disorders. Today the Menninger Foundation and the C. F. Menninger Hospital are considered the world leaders in psychiatric research and care for adults and children.

Spirits of the Plains

Father Juan de Padilla, who accompanied Coronado's expedition in search of Quivira in 1541, is often credited with being the first Christian religious leader in Kansas. After returning to Mexico with

Coronado, Father de Padilla decided to travel back north. He was killed in 1542 by the Indians he tried to convert to Christianity.

In 1824, Benton Pixley set up a mission among the Osage in present-day Neosho County. Six years later, Thomas Johnson opened the Shawnee Methodist Mission near Turner in present-day Wyandotte County. Isaac McCoy established a number of missions and schools for native people, including the Shawnee Baptist Mission in 1831.

Many immigrants came to Kansas more to hold onto their religions than to share them with others. Mennonites, Quakers, Dunkards (German Baptists), Eastern Orthodox Jews, and River Brethren moved into central Kansas. In Stafford County, Mormons (members of the Church of Jesus Christ of Latter-day Saints) started a colony called Zion Valley, and Irish Catholics founded Atwood.

More Kansans followed Roman Catholicism in 1990

St. Benedictine Church in Atchison

The Medicine Bundle

The most sacred objects possessed by Native Americans were their protective "medicine bundles." These bundles contained objects believed to have spiritual powers. Once a man had proven his abilities as a warrior, he was entitled to carry a medicine bundle. Plains Indians often used the bundles in important rituals and ceremonies. ∎

than any other religion. Methodists are the largest Protestant denomination. Disciples of Christ, Baptist, and Lutheran are also large Protestant denominations in Kansas. Other faiths are being introduced in Kansas today as immigrants continue to arrive from all over the world.

Caring for the Environment

Kansans generate less municipal waste per person than the people in most other states. Kansas ranks thirtieth out of all the states in the amount of hazardous waste it releases. However, people in Kansas have several environmental concerns. Some water wells are contaminated by nitrates from agricultural runoff. Toxic chemicals are regularly injected underground as part of the operation of the state's many oil- and gas-injection wells. So, while the air is considered some of the cleanest in the nation, the water quality is ranked as the lowest by some surveys.

"The people of Kansas have many decisions to make as citizens of the global community," Governor Graves declares. "Taking care of our natural resources in Kansas must always be one of our top priorities."

Still Coming

It was a typically windy Kansas day in 1878 when S. H. Carpenter arrived by train in Lawrence. He had come to serve as chancellor of the University of Kansas. Carpenter got off the train, looked around, and immediately got back on the train and left.

Millions of people are still coming to "look around" Kansas,

but unlike Carpenter, these visitors like what they see. Tourists spend $2 billion each year in Kansas, and many of them decide to make Kansas their home. A 1997 survey named Kansas the sixth most livable state in the nation.

Sunset at the Cheyenne Bottoms Wildlife Area.

CHAPTER TEN

Culture and Competition

Great writers, acclaimed artists, famous actors, versatile musicians, and legendary sports figures have contributed to the unique character and image of Kansas. Ask Kansans to define the state in one word, and they will most likely say "proud." The state is shaping the future without forgetting its rich cultural and competitive heritage.

Laura Ingalls Wilder

Kansas Architecture

Laura Ingalls Wilder's autobiography, *Little House on the Prairie*, which depicts happiness and hardship on the Kansas plains, became a hit television series. The Ingalls's log house was typical of Kansas's pioneer architecture, which is being preserved whenever possible.

Most of the first homes of settlers in Kansas were simply dug out of the earth. Others were made of sod bricks. These homes usually had only one or two rooms, with a fireplace where all the cooking was done. Light came from candles or oil lamps. Few original sod dugouts or cabins remain in Kansas today. Some of America's outstanding writers, musicians, and artists, however, came from these humble dwellings.

Kansas classic architecture includes gas stations built in the shapes of icebergs in Ottawa and tepees in Lawrence. Buildings designed by nineteenth-century architect John Gideon Haskell are still very visible. Haskell's courthouses in Douglas and Chase

Opposite: Kansan Gwendolyn Brooks with a portrait of herself

County are still used by county governments today. Kansas preservationists are working hard to save some of the state's most endangered pieces of architecture.

Kansas Writers

Lawrence-born writer Sara Paretsky's novels featuring detective V. I. Warshawski are among recent best-sellers by Kansas authors. William Least Heat-Moon's epic, *PrairyErth*, has made Chase County a familiar place to millions of readers around the world. Both writers credit Kansas for their inspiration, just as Pedro de Casteneda de Najera was inspired to write about Kansas in his journal during his travels with Spanish explorer Coronado so long ago.

The first factual book about Kansas, *Kanzas and Nebraska*, was written by Edward Everett Hale. He became widely known for his short story "The Man without a Country" during the Civil War. The first novel to be written with Kansas as a setting was written by Emerson Bennett and was published in 1857. It was called *The Border River.* In 1885, the humorous and serious poems of Eugene F. Ware, writing under the pseudonym "Ironquill," were published. Ernest Hemingway lived in Kansas while working on *A Farewell to Arms*, published in 1929.

L. Frank Baum's fictional *The Wizard of Oz* and Wilder's *Little House on the Prairie* are extremely different stories. They have one thing in common, however: both are the result of their authors' unforgettable experiences in Kansas.

Kansas-born authors Edgar Watson Howe, Edgar Lee Masters, Dorothy Canfield Fisher, and Damon Runyan became famous

Dorothy Canfield Fisher

for their abilities to explore the daily lives of ordinary people. Langston Hughes's novel, *Not without Laughter,* describes his youth growing up as a black boy in Kansas. Playwright William Gibson helped establish Kansas's reputation for inspiring the best in dramatic works with *The Miracle Worker*, a play based upon the life of Helen Keller. Charles M. Sheldon spent several years as a pastor in Kansas. His book *In His Steps* has become one of the best-selling books of all times.

Contemporary Kansas authors such as Paul Wellman (*The Comancheros*) and Gordon Parks (*The Learning Tree*) have seen their books become hit films. Jessie Lee Brown Foveaux of Manhattan is Kansas's most unusual contemporary author. In 1997, the ninety-eight-year-old writer received a $1 million advance from Warner Brothers for the film rights to her autobiography.

Music in the Air

Native American musicians were playing their drums and other instruments in Kansas long before the first European immigrants arrived with fiddles, guitars, and harmonicas. Musical Kansans today are famous for classical, contemporary, country, jazz, rock,

Kansas Jazz Legends

Eva Jessye (above) (1895–1979) has been dubbed the female dean of black music in America. Born in Coffeyville, Jessye gained fame as a singer, composer, and arranger who used spirituals as the basis of her music.

Stan Kenton (1912–1979) was born in Wichita and performed as an orchestra leader and jazz pianist all over the world. Millions of his recordings have been sold.

Charlie Parker (1920–1955), better known as Bird or Yardbird, was a Kansas City–born bebop saxophone player. Parker's fans say his style has often been imitated, but never matched. ▨

and pop compositions and performances. Opera singer Samuel Ramey of Colby, one of today's most popular stars of opera and the concert stage and the most-recorded American bass in history, and the rock band Kansas are examples of broad range of musical styles. The group Kansas, which formed in 1970, is still going strong.

The Wichita Symphony Orchestra, the Kansas City Symphony, and the National Guitar Flat-Picking Championships held at Winfield are also examples of the diversity of music attracting large audiences in Kansas. Other music festivals include the Baxoje Fall Encampment Pow Wow on the Iowa Reservation, Fiesta Mexicana in Topeka, and the Neewollah (that's "Halloween" spelled backward) Festival in Independence. And every Easter, singers in Lindsborg perform Handel's *Messiah* just as they have done each year since it was first performed there in 1880.

Visual Arts

A tractor instead of a brush, and seeds instead of paint: these are the tools of Kansas crop artist Stan Herd. While growing up on a Kansas farm, Herd plowed the soil and wondered how the fields looked from above. Herd wonders no more. By combining his artistic and farming skills, he has completed portraits on huge canvases of farmland. Whether viewed from the air or on the covers of national magazines, Herd's crop art has become symbolic of the unique expressions of modern Kansas artists.

The murals done in the late 1930s by Jefferson County's John Steuart Curry on the second floor of the state capitol were unique as well as controversial because of his depictions of abolitionist

John Brown. Curry's commission was canceled by the legislature due to the controversies. The paintings were eventually completed in 1978 by Belpre native Lumen Martin Winter. Curry also did sculptures of a white buffalo and a Native American on horseback for the state historical society's Kansas Museum of History, which opened in 1985.

Robert Merrell Gage's sculpture, *The Pioneer Woman,* on the capitol grounds has inspired other sculptural tributes to women pioneers. On the lawn of the Doniphan County Courthouse is the Tall Oak Indian Monument, a burr oak sculpture honoring Native Americans that stands 35 feet (10.7 m) high and weighs about 10 tons. It is the twenty-ninth sculpture in Peter Wolf Toth's Trail of the Whispering Giants series of fifty sculptures, one in each of the states.

Smokey Bear, the U.S. Forest Service mascot

Kansas cartoonist Mort Walker's syndicated comic strips appear in hundreds of newspapers. *Beetle Bailey* and *Hi and Lois* are enormously popular with cartoon fans of all ages. Some of Kansas's other artists are not as well known, but their creations are familiar to millions. For example, Rawlins County resident Rudolph Wendelen frequently drew Smokey Bear, the mascot of the U.S. Forest Service.

TV's Dodge City

The most popular Western ever to appear on television is *Gunsmoke*. It began as a radio program in 1952 with actor William Conrad reading the part of Marshal Matt Dillon. *Gunsmoke* debuted on television in 1955, with James Arness (right) as Matt Dillon, Amanda Blake as Miss Kitty Russell, and Milburn Stone as Doc Adams. These and other fictitional characters living in Dodge City during the cow town days remain so popular after the program's incredible twenty-year television run that repeats of the episodes are still being shown.

Gunsmoke holds the record for the largest number of episodes (635) among prime-time series with continuing characters. It has also been shown in other countries around the world. Many visitors to Kansas are surprised to learn there never was a real Dodge City marshal named Matt Dillon. ◾

Kansas Sports Stars

The game of basketball was born in Springfield, Massachusetts, but Kansas claims a strong tie to the early history of the sport. Shortly after establishing basketball in the East, the game's inventor, Dr. James Naismith (1861–1939), was hired as the University of Kansas's athletic director in 1898; he quickly set up a basketball team at the school, and suddenly basketball fever spread throughout the Midwest.

Dr. James Naismith

Naismith was succeeded as basketball coach in 1907 by Forrest "Phog" Allen. "Clean sports, next to religion, is the greatest thing on earth." That's the way Coach Allen concluded each of his popular radio sports shows. Now considered a basketball legend, Allen coached the Kansas Jayhawks for a total of 39 years, leading the team to three national championships.

Phog's promotion of athletic competition is one of the reasons Kansans have become famous, not only in basketball, but in almost every kind of sport. From preschool soccer games, to major-league football and baseball games, to the Wichita Wings professional soccer team and the Wichita Thunder professional hockey team, Kansans shine in the sport's spotlight.

Hoop Whoops

One of the country's most spirited rivalries in college basketball has been between the University of Kansas (KU) and Kansas State. Both schools made it into the NCAA's final eight in 1988, and the KU team, led by Danny Manning, won the championship.

In the mid-1950s, the University of Kansas campus was graced by perhaps the greatest basketball center of all time, Wilt Chamberlain (1936–). In college and the pros, Wilt the Stilt (as he was nicknamed) helped to revolutionize basketball into a game dominated by powerful centers who dunked the ball through the hoop. Chamberlain won four NBA MVP awards and was inducted into the Basketball Hall of Fame in 1978.

Women's basketball is popular at both the high school and college level in Kansas. Lynette Woodard (1959–) was the first woman at the University of Kansas to receive the college athlete Top Ten Award. Through her four All-American seasons at KU she set a scoring record of 3,640 points. Woodard captained the U.S. Olympic team that earned its first gold medal in women's basketball in 1984. She became the first woman ever to play for the Harlem Globetrotters professional basketball team.

Other Kansas hoopsters who have achieved national fame include Dave Stallworth, Jo Jo White, and Annette Wiles. Wiles played for the Lady Tigers of Fort Hays State, winners of the women's National Association of Intercollegiate Athletics (NAIA) championship in 1991.

Gayle Sayers

Football Fever

While James Naismith is well known as the inventor of basketball, few people know that he also invented the football helmet. Naismith reportedly came up with the idea of a helmet after having to cover his sore ear with tape before a game.

Among Kansas's most famous native football heroes are Gayle "The Kansas Comet" Sayers, who became the youngest player ever enshrined in the Pro Football Hall of Fame after playing for the Chicago Bears, and Barry Sanders, who won the 1988 Heisman Trophy. John Riggins, Ron Kramer, and

John Hadl are just a few of the Kansans who had made headlines with their pigskin skills. Kansas football fans flock to watch the Kansas City Chiefs play in the National Football League at Arrowhead Stadium in nearby Kansas City, Missouri.

Perhaps no sports story is as impressive as the phenomenal rise of Kansas State University's football program. The school's teams came from among the lowest rankings in the nation in the early 1990s to contention for the national championship in 1998.

George Brett

Diamond Stars

Whether they play for the American League Kansas City Royals or for other major-league teams, Kansas baseball players sparkle on the diamond. Elwood "Bingo" DeMoss, John Matlack, Bill Russell, Joe Tinker, Ray Sadeckie, George Brett, and Steve Renko are some of Kansas's baseball legends.

However, the sports world agrees that Coffeyville's Walter "Big Train" Johnson (1887–1946) has to be the greatest baseball pitcher of all times. Johnson won 417 major-league games for the Washington Senators, more than any other pitcher in American League history. He threw 110 shutouts, the most ever in the major leagues. Johnson was one of the first players elected to the Baseball Hall of Fame in 1936.

Ten Kansas Champions

- Professional golfer Tom Watson learned to play at Shawnee Mission.
- Pilot Harold Krier was the 1968 World Aerobatic Champion.
- Bill Koch won sailing's prestigious America's Cup in 1992.
- Michael Eglinski won the U.S. championship twice in orienteering, a sport that combines long-distance running and compass skills.
- Roger Ward won the Indianapolis 500 in 1959 and 1962.
- Marilyn Smith won twenty-two victories on the Ladies Professional Golf Association circuit.
- Jess Willard won the World Heavyweight Boxing Championship in 1915.
- Ted Allen set the horseshoe pitching record in 1951, tossing seventy-two ringers in a row.
- Ken Roberts was the World Champion Bull Rider in 1943, 1944, and 1945.
- Rick Mears has won the Indianapolis 500 four times: 1979, 1984, 1988, and 1991.

In 1989, Wichita State won the NCAA College World Series. Wichita is also home of the annual national semipro baseball tournament. It isn't unusual for one or more Kansas teams to be in the playoffs.

Other Arenas

Motor sports have been top attractions in Kansas since 1914. That year a dirt track in Dodge City became the site of the first 300-mile (483-km) motorcycle race in the United States. The first National Hot Rod Association (NHRA) nationals were held on an airstrip at Great Bend. Today, NHRA drag races bring spectators and competitors from around the world to Kansas.

Rick Mears

Shooting sports are extremely popular in Kansas. The state ranks among the top three states for pheasant and bobwhite quail hunting.

The most frequently attended professional sporting events in the state are thoroughbred horse racing and greyhound dog racing. Rodeos are also top attractions in Kansas. One of the largest Professional Rodeo Cowboy Association state rodeos is held annually in Dodge City.

Kansas runners Glenn Cunningham, Archie San Romani, Wes Santee, and Jim Ryun have each set world records in the mile run during their careers. Discus thrower Al Oerter, javelin thrower

Sam Colson, and shot-put stars Bill Nieder and Karl Salb hold the records in their respective sports, as does long jumper Ernie Shelby.

"Kansans long ago learned the importance of teamwork," wrote William Allen White in one of his newspaper editorials. "Whether building cities, playing baseball, or helping to win a world war, you can count on Kansans."

Timeline

United States History		Kansas State History

United States History

The first permanent English settlement is established in North America at Jamestown.	**1607**
Pilgrims found Plymouth Colony, the second permanent English settlement.	**1620**
America declares its independence from Britain.	**1776**
The Treaty of Paris officially ends the Revolutionary War in America.	**1783**
The U.S. Constitution is written.	**1787**
The Louisiana Purchase almost doubles the size of the United States.	**1803**
The United States and Britain fight the War of 1812.	**1812–15**
The North and South fight each other in the American Civil War.	**1861–65**

Kansas State History

1541	Francisco Vásquez de Coronado is the first recorded European to travel through Kansas.
1682	René-Robert Cavelier, Sieur de La Salle, claims for France all land drained by the Mississippi River; this includes what is now Kansas.
1803	Most of Kansas is purchased by the United States as part of the Louisiana Purchase.
1804	Lewis and Clark arrive at the Kansas River on June 26.
1822	The Santa Fe Trail is established by William Becknell.
1835	*The Shawnee Sun* is the first newspaper printed in the Shawnee language.
1854	Kansas is organized as a territory.
1855–61	Territorial conflicts rage and the state becomes known as Bleeding Kansas.

United States History

The United States is **1917–18**
involved in World War I.

The stock market crashes, **1929**
plunging the United States into
the Great Depression.

The United States **1941–45**
fights in World War II.
The United States becomes a **1945**
charter member of the U.N.

The United States **1951–53**
fights in the Korean War.

The U.S. Congress enacts a series of **1964**
groundbreaking civil rights laws.

The United States **1964–73**
engages in the Vietnam War.

The United States and other **1991**
nations fight the brief
Persian Gulf War against Iraq.

Kansas State History

1859 The Atchison, Topeka and Santa Fe
Railroad is chartered in Kansas.
1860 Oil is discovered near Paola in eastern
Kansas.
1861 Kansas becomes the thirty-fourth state
on January 29.

1864 The only Civil War battle fought in
Kansas occurs at Mine Creek on
October 25.

1910 The first electrical wire is connected
between Atchison and Tonganoxie.

1920 Natural gas is discovered near Liberal.

1932–39 Dust storms throughout the state
dry out the soil and ruin crops.

1954 The U.S. Supreme Court rules school
segregation unconstitutional in the
Brown v. *Board of Education* case,
which originated in Topeka.

1980 Kansas becomes the first state to fund
programs preventing child abuse.

Fast Facts

Kansas state capitol

Statehood date	January 29, 1861, the 34th state
Origin of state name	Sioux word for people of the "south wind"
State capital	Topeka
State nickname	Sunflower State, Jayhawk State
State motto	*Ad Astra per Aspera* (To the Stars through Difficulties)
State bird	Western meadowlark
State flower	Wild sunflower
State animal	American buffalo
State insect	Honeybee
State song	"Home on the Range "
State tree	Eastern cottonwood
State reptile	Ornate box turtle
State amphibian	Barred tiger salamander
State fair	Mid-September at Hutchinson
Total area; rank	82,282 sq. mi. (213,110 sq km); 15th
Land; rank	81,823 sq. mi. (211,922 sq km); 13th
Water; rank	459 sq. mi. (1,189 sq km); 40th
***Inland water;* rank**	459 sq. mi. (1,189 sq km); 34th
Geographic center	Barton, 15 miles (24 km) northeast of Great Bend

Ornate box turtle

Scott Lake

Flint Hills

Latitude and longitude	Kansas is located approximately between 37° 00′ and 40° 00′ N and 94° 37′ and 102° 03′ W
Highest point	Mount Sunflower, 4,039 feet (1,231 m)
Lowest point	Verdigris River, 680 feet (207 m)
Largest city	Wichita
Number of counties	105
Population; rank	2,485,600 (1990 census); 32nd
Density	30 persons per sq. mi. (12 per sq km)
Population distribution	69% urban, 31% rural

Ethnic distribution (does not equal 100%)

White	90.09%
African-American	5.77%
Hispanic	3.78%
Asian and Pacific Islanders	1.28%
Other	1.97%
Native American	0.089%

Record high temperature	121°F (49°C) at Fredonia on July 18, 1936, and near Alton on July 24, 1936
Record low temperature	–40°F (–40°C) at Lebanon on February 13, 1905
Average July temperature	78°F (26°C)
Average January temperature	30°F (–1°C)
Average annual precipitation	27 inches (69 cm)

At the U.S. geographic center

Natural Areas and Historic Sites

National Historic Sites

Brown v. Board of Education National Historic Site commemorates the Supreme Court decision that led to the end of racial segregation in U.S. schools. The site is the Monroe Elementary School, which Linda Brown attended.

Fort Larned National Historic Site is the site of a military outpost built midway along the Santa Fe Trail to protect both mail and travelers.

Fort Scott National Historic Site is the site of a nineteenth-century frontier military base for the U.S. Army.

State Parks

Kansas maintains twenty-five state parks and recreation areas.

Sports Teams

NCAA Teams (Division 1)

Kansas State University Wildcats

University of Kansas Jayhawks

Wichita State University Shockers

Cultural Institutions

Libraries

The Kansas State Library in Topeka provides information on the Kansas state government to the general public and public officials.

The Kansas State Historical Society in Topeka, in existence since 1875, has a large amount of material on Kansas history and holds one of the nation's largest state newspaper collections.

The Wichita Public Library system offers services to the public and holds many events, such as author readings, storytimes, and lectures.

George Brett

Old Castle Museum

Museums

The Wichita Art Museum has a large collection of American art, including works by Mary Cassatt, John Singleton Copley, and Edward Hopper. It also hosts many exhibits throughout the year.

The Kansas Cosmosphere and Space Center in Hutchinson holds the Hall of Space Museum, displaying one of the largest collection of space suits and other space memorabilia in the world.

The Old Allen County Jail and Museum Gallery in Iola gives tours of a prison built eight years after Kansas's statehood in 1861. Visitors can see a solitary confinement cell, cell cage, and lots of graffiti from the late nineteenth century.

Performing Arts

Kansas has one major symphony orchestra.

Universities and Colleges

In the mid-1990s, Kansas had twenty-nine public and twenty-two private institutions of higher education.

Annual Events

January–March

International Pancake Derby in Liberal (Shrove Tuesday)

National Junior College Basketball Tournament in Hutchinson (third week in March)

Kansas Special Olympics in Wichita (last week in March)

Messiah Festival in Lindsborg (Holy Week)

April–June

Kansas Relays in Lawrence (April)

National Coursing Meet (greyhound racing) near Abilene (mid-April)

Eisenhower Center Open House in Abilene (late April)

Wichita River Festival in Wichita (mid-May)

Native American festival

All Schools Day in McPherson (mid-May)

Beef Empire Days in Garden City (early June)

Flint Hills Rodeo in Strong City (early June)

Midsummer's Day Festival in Lindsborg (June)

July–September

National Space Week at the Cosmosphere and Space Center in Hutchinson (July)

Mexican Fiesta in Topeka (July)

Days of '49 in Hanover (July)

Kickapoo Indian Powwow in Topeka (late July)

Czech Festival and Arts and Crafts Show in Wilson (late July)

Dodge City Days (late July)

County fairs and rodeos in many cities (August)

National Baseball Congress Tournament in Wichita (August)

North Central Kansas Fair in Belleville (first week in September)

Kansas State Fair in Hutchinson (mid-September)

National Flat-Picking Guitar Championships and Bluegrass Festival in Winfield (third week in September)

October–December

Pioneer Christmas Arts and Crafts Festival in Wichita (November)

St. Lucia Festival in Lindsborg (December)

Christmas at the Art Museum in Wichita (December)

Hula hoop contest

Famous People

Gwendolyn Elizabeth Brooks (1917–)	Poet
John Brown (1800–1859)	Abolitionist
Wilt Chamberlain (1936–)	Basketball player

Amelia Earhart

Walter Percy Chrysler (1875–1940)	Automobile manufacturer
William "Buffalo Bill" Cody (1846–1917)	Entertainer and explorer
John Steuart Curry (1897–1946)	Painter
Robert Joseph Dole (1923–)	Politician
Amelia Mary Earhart (1897–1937?)	Aviator
Dwight David Eisenhower (1890–1969)	U.S. president
James "Wild Bill" Hickok (1837–1876)	Law officer and Union scout
Dennis Hopper (1936–)	Actor
Nancy Kassebaum (1932–)	Politician
Damon Runyon (1884–1946)	Journalist and author
Susanna M. Salter (1860–1961)	Politician
Gayle Eugene Sayers (1943–)	Football player
William Allen White (1868–1944)	Editor and publisher

To Find Out More

History

- Chu, Daniel, and Bill Shaw. *Going Home to Nicodemus: The Story of an African-American Frontier Town and the Pioneers Who Settled It.* New York: Julian Messner, 1995.

- Duey, Kathleen. *Willow Chase: Kansas Territory, 1847.* American Diaries, No 5. New York: Aladdin, 1997.

- Fradin, Dennis Brindell. *Kansas.* Chicago: Childrens Press, 1995.

- Fredeen, Charles. *Kansas.* Minneapolis: Lerner, 1992.

- Stratton, Joanna. *Pioneer Women Voices from the Kansas Frontier.* New York: Simon and Schuster, 1981.

- Thompson, Kathleen. *Kansas.* Austin, Tex.: Raintree/Steck Vaughn, 1996.

Biographies

- Cwiklik, Robert, and W. David Baird. *Tecumseh: Shawnee Rebel.* Broomall, Penn.: Chelsea House, 1993.

- Jacobs, William J. *Coronado: Dreamer in Golden Armor.* New York: Franklin Watts, 1994.

Fiction

- Baum, Frank L. *The Wizard of Oz.* New York: Henry Holt, 1988.

- MacLachlan, Patricia. *Sarah, Plain and Tall.* New York: HarperCollins, 1985.

Websites

- **Kansas State Website**
  http://www.state.ks.us
  The official state website

- **Kansas State University Libraries**
  http://www.lib.ksu.edu.
  A listing of libraries and library information for Kansas State University

- **Dwight D. Eisenhower Library**
  http://redbud.lbjlib.utexas. edu/eisenhower/ CONTENTS.htm
  The website to Eisenhower's presidential library

- **Blue Skyways**
  http://skyways.lib.ks.us/
  Supported by the state library, this site leads to cultural and informational links all over Kansas

Addresses

- **Kansas Department of Commerce**
  Travel and Tourism Division
  700 S.W. Harrison
  Suite 1300
  Topeka, KS 66603
  For information about travel and tourism in Kansas

- **Kansas Department of Commerce**
  Development Division
  700 S.W. Harrison
  Suite 1300
  Topeka, KS 66603
  For information about Kansas's economy

- **Division of Legislative Administrative Services**
  511-S State House
  Topeka, KS 66612
  For information about government in Kansas

- **Kansas State Historical Society**
  120 W. 10th Street
  Topeka, KS 66612
  For information about Kansas history

Index

Page numbers in *italics* indicate illustrations.

Meet the Author

Nancy Robinson Masters is a pilot, explorer, and author who has been writing about people, places, and planes for more than twenty years. She grew up on a farm in Jones County, Texas, and began her professional writing career as a high-school student.

"I wanted to take flying lessons. I began selling stories to magazines and newspapers and told all of my friends I was saving the money I earned to someday buy an airplane."

"Someday" for Nancy came almost ten years and hundreds of published articles later. Her first trip as a licensed pilot took her to Kansas, and she's been going back ever since. Nancy currently travels throughout America presenting visiting-author programs for schools, and programs for businesses and civic organizations motivating people to read and to write. She is also the author of *Georgia* in the America the Beautiful series.

Nancy logged many hours writing *Kansas*. She says the best part of writing this book "was hearing all the stories the people of Kansas shared with me. The hardest part about writing this book was not being able to include all of those stories."

Nancy and her husband, veteran aviator Bill Masters, live on a farm in Elmdale near Abilene, Texas, with their four dogs and four cats. Her goal is to "keep climbing, and to encourage students to do the same if they want to achieve their dreams."

Photo Credits